K. Marx & F. Engels:

On Colonies, Industrial Monopoly and the Working Class Movement

Originally compiled and edited by the
Communist Working Circle (CWC), 1972

Introduction by Zak Cope
and Torkil Lauesen, 2016

Karl Marx and Friedrich Engels: On Colonies, Industrial Monopoly and the Working Class Movement

ISBN: 978-1-894946-79-7

This edition copyright 2016 Kersplebedeb

Edited by Revolutionary Anti-Imperialist Movement, 2016
Revolutionaryaim.org

Kersplebedeb Publishing
CP 63560
CCCP Van Horne
Montreal, Quebec
Canada H3W 3H8

info@kersplebedeb.com
www.kersplebedeb.com
www.leftwingbooks.net

Copies available from:

AK Press
370 Ryan Avenue #100
Chico, CA
95973

Voice: (510) 208-1700
Fax: (510) 208-1701
www.akpress.org

PRINTED IN CANADA

Contents:

1 Revolutionary Anti-Imperialist Movement: Foreword

5 Zak Cope and Torkil Lauesen: Introduction

63 Karl Marx: The Poverty of Philosophy

64 Karl Marx and Friedrich Engels: Manifesto of the Communist Party

67 Karl Marx and Friedrich Engels: Address of the Central Committee to the Communist League

69 Karl Marx: Revolution in China and in Europe

73 Karl Marx: The British Rule in India

78 Karl Marx: The Future Results of the British Rule in India

82 Letter from Engels to Marx, May 23, 1856

87 Karl Marx: English Ferocity in China

89 Friedrich Engels: Persia and China

90 Letter from Engels to Marx, October 7, 1858

92 Letter from Marx to Engels, November 17, 1862

93 Karl Marx: Capital, Vol. I, Chapter XXXI

96 Letter from Marx to Engels, November 30, 1867

99 Letter from Marx to Kugelmann, April 6, 1868

101 Letter from Engels to Marx, November 18, 1868

103 Letter from Engels to Marx, October 24, 1869

104 Letter from Marx to Kugelmann, November 29, 1869

107 Letter from Marx to Engels, December 10, 1869

108 Letter from Marx to Meyer and Vogt, April 9, 1870

115 Friedrich Engels: The English Elections

119 Letter from Marx to Liebknecht, February 11, 1878

120 Letter from Engels to Bernstein, June 17, 1879

122 Letter from Marx to Danielson, February 19, 1881

123 Letter from Engels to Kautsky, September 12, 1882

125 Letter from Engels to Bebel, August 30, 1883

128 Friedrich Engels: England in 1845 and in 1885

139 Letter from Engels to Bebel, October 28, 1885

141 Letter from Engels to Sorge, December 7, 1889

143 Letter from Engels to Sorge, April 19, 1890

145 Letter from Engels to Kautsky, September 4, 1892

147 Letter from Engels to Sorge, January 18, 1893

149 Letter from Engels to Plekhanov, May 21, 1894

Foreword

By Revolutionary Anti-Imperialist Movement

We would like to start by expressing our tremendous gratitude to all involved for their combined effort to bring this project to fruition. The prodigious amount of work associated with editing, formatting, and design undertaken by many comrades, made this project possible. Originally compiled by the Communist Working Group (CWC) (Danish *Kommunistisk Arbejdskreds*, KAK), the selections which follow, taken from published material as well as private correspondence, show us Marx and Engels as they confront the greatest strategic problem of their—as well as our—time: the complication of class-struggle by the differential effect of colonialism between the oppressor and oppressed nations.

Since the First International, Marxists have grappled with this problem—sometimes opportunistically and other times creatively—and now more than ever, more than two decades after the End of History, and as the world veers towards crisis and multipolarity, it is of paramount importance. We do not approach this project lightly. The left, whether in the core or the periphery, gains nothing from pretending that the horizons of struggle for

---

The Revolutionary Anti-Imperialist Movement (RAIM) is a collective of revolutionary communist organizers, activists, artists, and technical workers based in the imperialist countries of Western Europe and North Amerika whose work deals mainly with engaging the revolutionary left on strategic and theoretical questions from a third-worldist perspective for the purpose of fostering the strategic thinking and theoretical creativity necessary to surmount problems of revolution in the core countries.

web: revolutionaryaim.org   email: revolutionaryaim@yandex.com the masses of the oppressor and oppressed nations are the same. In fact, they stand to lose bitterly by doing so. For our part, the Revolutionary Anti-Imperialist Movement has worked to raise consciousness on this question, gather like-minded Marxists and sympathizers into discussion and study, and to engage the stagnant left in north amerika on questions of the labor aristocracy, opportunism, chauvinism, internal colonization and more, with mixed results. On the one hand, we have succeeded in changing the timbre of discussion broadly from Marxist-Leninist to Maoist to anarchist circles, forcing many of these formations to the left on these questions. On the other, such engagement has its limits, and events (domestic prison and colonial rebellions, the possibility of major new wars, the rise of popular labor-aristocratic revanchism in the overdeveloped countries) are quickly outpacing these efforts. Since many of us began work with RAIM, a decided shift in the language that has characterized all discussion of parasitism, opportunism, and chauvinism has been observed. Just a few years ago all of these ideas were either absent from, or mocked by, the majority of left discourse. Now, when these concepts are not being adopted by our former critics—usually in shallow and underdeveloped ways—and passed off as if they are natural conclusions unworthy of so much attention, they are furiously attacked and denounced as anti-people, anti-masses, etc. This is nonetheless a positive development. If left unstirred, unchallenged, if left to languish in pre-modern and morbid theoretical states, Marxism becomes nothing but necromancy—calling to the dead to divine your future.

Creativity—the ability to recognize, absorb and synthesize new developments in the political terrain and strategize around them toward final victory—is the real living, scientific core of Marxism. Now, long after the victory of capitalist restoration in Asia and Europe, the left is free from the shackles of great power rivalries, but it is also more divided than ever. It is not equipped in the least to defend itself against the allure of opportunism and the populist violence of the labor aristocracy and the settler masses, let alone to channel the popular rage of those strategic ulcers in the belly of the beast—black/New Afrikan, Xicanx, and Indigenous resistance, as well as sizable numbers (but by no means approaching a majority) of workers and students of the oppressor nation uninterested in bribery—to form a true revolutionary nucleus that can raise the struggle against internal colonization and imperialism to a new level. Will we, the communist left, remain a tiny, atomized minority, able only to coordinate disruptions to this or that outrage and perhaps exhort ourselves to the occasional meaningful act of internationalist solidarity, until the day imperialism's global tentacles are cut? Then we must organize and prepare for that. Or will multipolarity, internal unrest, imperialist war, world crisis, and upheavals in the periphery open up a qualitatively new window of opportunity for us? Then we must prepare and organize for that, too.

Whatever develops, we must meet it with discipline, unity and, above all, correct theory. For this reason, we thank Kersplebedeb immensely for publishing such a wide array of materials with an anti-imperialist, anti-chauvinist, and anti-opportunist emphasis, without which so much of the material foundational to not only our organization, but to a massive and fruitful movement-wide discussion, would be unavailable. Similarly, we thank Dr. Cope for his immense and ongoing contributions to the political economy of anti-imperialism—so far most comprehensively in *Divided World Divided Class*, now in its second edition—and for his work on this project. And Torkil Lauesen, former member of CWC (the original publishers of the bulk of the present work) and M-KA, whose contributions to this global discussion are dwarfed only by the mind-boggling acts of solidarity which he and his comrades are responsible for (the best, and pretty much only, English-language resource for which is the astounding *Turning Money Into Rebellion: The Unlikely Story of Denmark's Revolutionary Bank Robbers*, edited by Gabriel Kuhn, and available from PM Press and Kersplebedeb).

We look forward to the positive contribution the present project stands to make to this discussion.

> Organizing Committee for the
> Revolutionary Anti-Imperialist Movement
> (RAIM-OC)

Introduction

By Zak Cope and Torkil Lauesen

This collection of texts by Marx and Engels on colonialism, industrial monopoly, and the labor movement is a reprint of a booklet published in 1972. The texts were originally collected by a Danish anti-imperialist group called the Communist Working Circle (CWC). In the late 1960s, the CWC developed the so-called "parasite state" (*"snylerstaten,"* literally "leech state") theory linking the imperialist exploitation and oppression of the proletariat in the global "South" with the establishment of states in the global "North" in which the working class lives in relative prosperity.

In connection with the CWC's studies of the development of this division of the world and of the global working class, they selected and published these texts by Marx and Engels under the title *On Colonies, Industrial Monopoly and the Labor Movement*. As the title indicates, the texts focus on the connection between colonialism, the establishment of an English industrial monopoly around the middle of the 19th century, and the consequent spread of bourgeois ideology within the English working class.

There is a tradition in ostensibly Marxist thought which prides itself on making the labor of hundreds and thousands of millions of slaves, peasants, and superexploited workers in the export dependencies and colonies disappear from the ledger sheets and pay packets of the advanced capitalist countries. By contrast, we argue that a section of the working class had and continues to have a vested interest in maintaining the profitability of capitalist enterprise, thus necessitating imperialism (first colonialism, and now neocolonialism). The dimensions of this labor aristocracy, undergirded by the superexploitation of the international proletariat, have expanded to encompass the overwhelming majority of metropolitan employees. The stratification of labor globally implies a relatively rigid caste-like system for which white nationalism is typically a basic organising principle (Cope 2014).

Primitive Accumulation

What are the main observations of Marx and Engels concerning the connection between colonialism, English industrial monopoly, and the spread of bourgeois ideology throughout the working class? First, Marx underlines the connection between the colonial plunder of Latin America, Africa, and Asia and the breakthrough of capitalism in Northwestern Europe. In the 17th and 18th centuries, the number of laborers and slaves in plantations, haciendas, factories, and mines in the colonies was at least as large as the proletariat of Europe itself (Blaut 1987, p. 181). The exploitation of the colonies created the wealth that made up the original capital that produced the breakthrough of industrial capitalism in England in the early 19th century. Marx describes this in *Capital*, in the chapter "The genesis of industrial capital" (page 93 in this book).

Blaut suggests two ways to assess the real significance of colonial production to the beginnings of capitalism in the 16th century. The first is to "trace the direct and indirect effects of colonialism on European society, looking for movements of goods and capital, tracing labor flows into industries and regions stimulated or created by colonial enterprise or closely connected to it, and the like"

(Blaut 1993, p. 193). The second "is to arrive at a global calculation of the amount of labor (free and unfree) that was employed in European enterprises in America, Africa, and Asia, along with the amount of labor in Europe itself which was employed in activities derived from extra-European enterprise, and then to look at these quantities in relation to the total labor market in Europe for economic activities that can be thought of as connected to the rise of capitalism" (ibid).

On the basis of population data, and noting the divergent rates of exploitation of labor, Blaut (1993, p. 194) argues that "the European populations were [no] more intimately involved in the rise of capitalism than the American populations—that is, the 13 million people who we assume were in European-dominated regions." Moreover, "It is likely that the proportion of the American population that was engaged in labor for Europeans, as wage work, as forced labor including slave labor, and as the labor of farmers delivering goods as tribute or rent in kind, was no lower than the proportion of Iberian people engaged in labor for commercialized sectors of the Spanish and Portuguese economy" (ibid).

Acemoglu et al (2002) have argued that the rise of Western Europe after 1500 "is due largely to growth in countries with access to the Atlantic Ocean and with substantial trade with the New World, Africa, and Asia via the Atlantic. This trade and the associated colonialism affected Europe not only directly, but also indirectly by inducing institutional change. Where "initial" political institutions (those established before 1500) placed significant checks on the monarchy, the growth of Atlantic trade strengthened merchant groups by constraining the power of the monarchy, and helped merchants obtain changes in institutions to protect property rights. These changes were central to subsequent economic growth." The authors further demonstrate that nearly all the differential growth of Western Europe between the 16th and early 19th centuries is accounted for by the growth of Atlantic trading nations directly involved in trade and colonialism with the New World and Asia, namely, Britain, France, the Netherlands, Portugal, and Spain, a pattern in large measure reflecting the direct effects of Atlantic trade between Europe and America, Africa and Asia.

The external precondition of Britain's growth as a capitalist country was commercial hegemony founded upon a burgeoning colonial empire. Britain became the center of world trade, and an industrial division of labor developed in relation to overseas countries. These supplied the raw materials for British industry, which in return supplied the finished products. Britain became the workshop of the world, and her industry expanded in an international setting created by the British navy. This hegemonic position guaranteed Britain a monopoly of industrial manufacture, a monopoly that it held through the first half of the 19th century. During this initial period, British capitalism developed at the expense of handicraft production nationally and internationally, ensuring that comparatively cheaper British industrial goods dominated the world market.

Marx and Engels on the Development of Capitalism

This situation was not to last, and the most serious economic depression capitalism had yet experienced materialized around 1873. As capitalism expanded, competing firms in the metropolitan countries endeavored to increase productivity using new industrial techniques. The discovery of electricity alongside scientific innovations in chemical and steel production (the so-called "second industrial revolution"), alongside the expansion of colonial and American agriculture, led to overproduction and a consequent fall in the prices of commodities. At the same time, the ratio between constant (c, raw materials and machinery) and variable capital (v, labor power, or wages), what Marx called the "organic composition of capital," has an ongoing tendency to expand. The combination of a rising organic composition of capital, rising wages, and intensified international competition accompanying the spread of industrialization in Germany and the United States, resulted in a glut in commodities markets, a regression in the rate of exploitation, and a decline in the rate of profit (that is the sum of surplus value (s) divided by total capital ($c + v$) outlay) (Cottrell [1980] 2006, pp. 262–4).

In the first half of the 19th century, it was difficult for capital to meet the demands of the proletariat if the rate of profit was to be maintained. During this period the productive forces were revolutionized. The advance from spinning wheel to spinning-machine, from handloom to power-loom, the invention of the steam engine, the introduction of the railways and so on, increased productivity exponentially. However, this increase in productivity did not in any way mean better conditions for the working class—on the contrary. During the whole period, wages were near the physiological subsistence level. Industry no longer competed only with handicrafts, but competition among the capitalists themselves became its most important form. Consequently, major demands for improvements were rejected. The bourgeoisie could not in this period afford the luxury of higher wages and better working conditions, not to mention universal male suffrage, the right to form trade unions, and other demands made by the English working class.

Reform at that time threatened the very existence of the capitalist system. The 1840s and 1850s were thus a period of chaotic conflict between labor and capital. The early labor movement developed new forms of action such as the strike and industrial sabotage. Citizens revolted in the streets of the big cities. This was met with harsh repression by the ruling elite which feared revolution and the "dangerous classes." In 1848, a wave of revolutionary uprisings swept through Europe's cities. It was in this context that Marx and Engels wrote in the first line of the *Communist Manifesto*: "There is a specter haunting Europe—the specter of communism."

The Colonialist Solution

In the mid-19th century, the system had only one way in which crises might be avoided, and that was to find new markets for goods and capital. Imperialism is in part the attempt to resolve the contradiction between production and consumption by creating a buoyant consumer market in the First World while at the same time relocating low-wage production to the Third World. Capitalism cannot be confined to one country; according to its very nature it must continuously expand. Marx and Engels describe this trend in *The Communist Manifesto* (see page 64 in this book). Marx regarded capitalist development as a centrifugal process driven by the contradictions of capitalism itself. These were manifested by the decreasing possibilities of profitable investment in the most highly developed capitalist countries. At the same time, more profitable investments could be made in the colonies and in the less developed countries.

Marx believed that the export of capital would result in capitalism spreading all over the world. However, he did not imagine that it would institute a rigid division of the world between a highly developed imperialist center and an exploited and underdeveloped periphery. Marx thought that capital would diffuse outwardly, making the rest of the world a reflected image of Britain, and thus develop the same contradictions globally as it had domestically, ones which threatened capitalism's existence and would thereby pave the way for a worldwide revolutionary socialist process. As Marx ([1867] 1954, p. 19) writes in *Capital*: "The country that is more developed industrially only shows, to the less developed, the image of its own future."

Around 1830, Britain had completed the initial stage of the industrial revolution. At that time, continental Europe and the United States had hardly begun theirs. These countries did not become a periphery to Britain. On the contrary, British capital contributed largely to making them highly developed capitalist countries. The United States caught up with Britain a few decades later. Marx believed that the development of capitalism in the colonized countries of Asia and Africa would be similar. When Britain had destroyed the original societies and introduced capitalism, these colonies would experience a rapid development. Marx describes this in August 1853 in his article "The future results of the British rule in India" in the newspaper *Daily Tribune* (page 78).

The opening of new markets in Africa and Asia, and the export of capital to North and South America would put off the collapse of capitalism for a while. However, it would only be a short respite; the final result would merely be an even more intense accumulation which would lead to a new and more intensified crisis of overproduction (Engels [1848] 1976, pp. 527–9). In fact, however, capitalism did spread out across the globe, but as a polarizing process, not only between the bourgeoisie and the working class, but also as a division between an imperialist center and an exploited periphery. This fundamental contradiction gave capitalism completely new conditions of growth and a longer life.

Marx and Engels's considerations regarding the development of the colonies and the early collapse of capitalism did not transpire. This is not to say that their analyses of capitalism at that time were wrong. In the middle of the 19th century, the capitalist system was indeed on the verge of having exhausted its potential. Crises arose at ever shorter intervals and assumed an increasingly serious character. The strength and fighting spirit of the proletariat grew accordingly: the "specter of communism" moved through Europe, materializing in the uprising of the Paris Commune of 1871. The bourgeoisie was terrified of revolution. What Marx and Engels could not foresee was that just when aggravating crises seemed to forebode terminal crisis, a new development offered it renewed strength and vigor, namely, the transfer of values from abroad.

Crucially, in Marxist terms, as a force to counteract the tendency for the rate of profit to fall, imperialism is of the highest import. Marx listed five major ways that this tendency is forestalled: (1) cheapening of the elements of constant capital (raw materials and machinery); (2) raising of the intensity of exploitation (longer working days and more efficient labor organisation); (3) depression of wages below their value (superexploitation, or the payment of less than the domestic average value of labor power); (4) relative overpopulation (or a larger reserve army of labor); and (5) foreign trade (Sweezy 1949, pp. 97–100). Every one of these countervailing forces is realized through imperialist exploitation of dependent nations.

Jawaharlal Nehru ([1934] 1982, p. 548), India's first Prime Minister, highlighted the significance of imperialism in a world history originally written for his daughter:

"It is said that capitalism managed to prolong its life to our day because of a factor which perhaps Marx did not fully consider. This was the exploitation of colonial empires by the industrial countries of the West. This gave fresh life and prosperity to it, at the expense, of course, of the poor countries so exploited."

From Dangerous Class to National Citizenship

In the second half of the 19th century, the conditions of the European proletariat slowly began to change. For the first time in the history of capitalism, the capitalists had to pay wages above the mere subsistence level. This first tiny improvement was not primarily a result of the fight of the proletariat itself. The labor movement was politically weaker than before and Chartism had been impaired by cleavage and corruption. Rather, these first improvements in wages and working conditions for the British proletariat were due to contradictions between rival factions of the ruling class.

As noted, Britain had a virtual monopoly of industrial goods at the beginning of the 19th century, resulting in extra profits. However, these profits did not only go to the industrial capitalists, and during the first part of the century it definitely did not result in higher real wages for the working class either. Paradoxically, a large portion of the extra profits from the industrial monopoly was passed on to the landowning class, its historically strong position in Parliament having allowed it to introduce an embargo on the import of corn and other agricultural products into Britain from 1804. The landowners could thereby maintain a high level of prices for their products ensuring that capitalists had to pay their workers comparatively high nominal wages just to enable them to live above the breadline.

By this artificially high price of corn the landowners could apportion to themselves a considerable part of the extra profits earned by Britain's industrial monopoly. Therefore, in the 1840s the industrial capitalists struggled to have the Corn Laws repealed. Allied with the working class they succeeded in 1846. The reopening of the importation of corn from Prussia and later from the United States caused a fall in the prices of bread and other food.

Following the fall in corn prices, the industrial capitalists tried to decrease wages, but the working class was able to limit this decrease and thus obtain an improvement. This victory was added to shortly after the abrogation of the Corn Laws, by the introduction of a ten-hour working day, a goal for which the workers had been fighting for thirty years. Here organized labor was unexpectedly supported by the landowners in Parliament, who thirsted for revenge on the industrial capitalists.

The extra profits of the British industrial monopoly and the internal fight between landowners and industrial capitalists meant that the wages of the British working class were increased above the subsistence level at which they had been so far kept. Between 1850 and 1872, imports of wheat more than doubled and imports of meat increased eightfold. Slowly the bourgeoisie changed its political strategy from repression of the "dangerous classes" to a gradual inclusion of the working class as national citizens. In the 1860s and 1870s both Napoleon III of France and the Conservative government in England allowed the working class to organize. Socialist parties were formed in all Western European countries while the trade union movement grew in strength. The right to vote was extended to include men from the working class, wage levels rose, and the first social and health insurance systems were introduced.

Parallel to this development was a de-radicalization of the Western European working class. It had left the 1848 revolutions and the Paris barricades behind in favor of parliamentarism and negotiation with employers. Class struggle became a controlled process within the parameters set by the system. Working-class political parties and trade unions successfully fought for higher wages and better working conditions, for unemployment and health insurance, pensions, and so forth. The result was a compromise between capital and the working class which dampened the future form class struggle would take.

This historic compromise had a dark side. The developing welfare services of the state, and the widening and deepening of the franchise, united the former "dangerous classes" behind the nation-state in imperialist wars. So that the citizens in the center of the Empire could enjoy a growing welfare, ideologies of "national interest" and racism arose to justify policies which, by contrast, meant death and misery for the people in the colonies. It is this that Australian academic M.G.E. Kelly calls "biopolitical imperialism."

"Imperialism, therefore, is primarily thanatopolitical, a politics of death, contrasting with the biopolitics of the population found within the metropole. There is, I will contend, a direct relation between the two things, in which death is figuratively exported and life imported back, in a systematic degradation of the possibilities for biopolitics in the periphery, arising out of the operation of biopolitics in the center. …

"I will argue that biopolitics constitutes a missing link in explaining how imperialism involves ordinary people of the First World. For one thing, biopolitics provides a mechanism by which the profits of imperialism may be spread to a whole population. By uniting us in a single population, moreover, biopolitics generates solidarity between ordinary people and elites." (Kelly 2015, pp. 18–19)

Mike Davis (2000, p. 59) illustrates this reality through case studies of India, China, and Brazil that show how imperialism in the form of direct governmental intervention or "neutral" economic processes destroys the health and welfare of these countries' populations:

INTRODUCTION

"Between 1875–1900—a period that included the worst famines in Indian history—annual grain exports increased from 3 to 10 million tons, equivalent to the annual nutrition of 25m people. Indeed, by the turn of the century, India was supplying nearly a fifth of Britain's wheat consumption at the cost of its own food security."

In addition India also had to pay a part of the British Empire's military effort in cash and lives:

"Already saddled with a huge public debt that included reimbursing the stockholders of the East India Company and paying the costs of the 1857 revolt, India also had to finance British military supremacy in Asia. In addition to incessant proxy warfare with Russia on the Afghan frontier, the subcontinent's masses also subsidized such far-flung adventures of the Indian Army as the occupation of Egypt, the invasion of Ethiopia, and the conquest of the Sudan. As a result, military expenditures never comprised less than 25 percent (34 percent including police) of India's annual budget" (ibid, pp. 60–1).

As an example of the restructuring of the local economy to suit imperial needs regardless of the consequences for the population in the colonies, Davis (ibid, p. 66) notes: "During the famine of 1899–1900, when 143,000 Beraris died directly from starvation, the province exported not only thousands of bales of cotton but an incredible 747,000 bushels of grain."

INTRODUCTION

The Rationale behind Capitalist Colonialism

During the 1850s, committed proponents of free trade considered that the costs of administering and enforcing British colonial diktat would outweigh any potential or actual economic benefits derived from it. For authors then and since, including those ostensibly opposed to formal colonialism, the colonising nations of Europe and North America did not substantially benefit from colonialism; rather, it was only a thin stratum of private investors, officials, and migrant workers who benefited.

During the early 19th century, there were precious few consistent free trade anti-imperialists, the most famous, manufacturer and Radical free trade supporter Richard Cobden, excepted. As Marx recognized in 1853, "when India had been in the process of annexation, everyone had kept quiet; once the 'natural limits' had been reached, they had 'become loudest with their hypocritical peace cant.' But, then, 'firstly, they had to get it [India] in order to subject it to their sharp philanthropy.' ... In 1859 Marx was writing that 'the "glorious" reconquest of India after the Mutiny' had been essentially carried out for securing the monopoly of the Indian market to the Manchester free traders" (Habib 2002, pp. 8–9).

Adam Smith is well-known for having insisted that colonies were a never-ending source of war and expense for the colonising country. Less well known is the fact that his opposition to colonialism was fundamentally based on opposition to colonial monopolies in trade and investment as opposed to colonialism *tout court*. For Smith, colonialism was permissible if the colony contributed net revenue to the metropolis within a system of free trade for all members of an Imperial Federation (Kittrell 1965, p. 49).

More recently, Thomas and McCloskey (1981) argue that the Empire was an overall burden on the British economy. For not only did Imperial preferential duties ensure that British consumers paid over the world market price for West Indian commodities like cotton, ginger, indigo, molasses, rum, pimento, and sugar (they neglect to discuss the purchasing power of British wages), but the costs of occupying and administering the colonies, not to mention defending them from rival colonial powers, were a severe drain on the British government budget.

Are these authors correct in their estimate of the negligible role of Empire in Britain's economy? According to economic historian Ralph Davis (1979, p. 10):

"Overseas trade did much to strengthen Britain's economic life during the eighteenth century, and in doing so it helped to create the base without which the industrial take-off might not have proceeded so fast or gone so far. Moreover, once home demand ceased to be sufficient to maintain the momentum of growth of the most advanced industries, around 1800, overseas trade did begin to play an absolutely vital direct part in their further expansion."

Indeed, there can be no doubt that colonialism was crucial to British and European capital accumulation. Imperialist trade and investment in the Third World is the foundation of the capitalist world economy, and not only historically. As the great historian and first Prime Minister of Trinidad and Tobago Eric Williams wrote: "The colonial system was the spinal cord of the commercial capitalism of the mercantile epoch" (Williams 1944, p. 142). In particular, the massive profits accruing from the slave trade and slave-based production were used to finance early British capital accumulation in shipping, insurance, agriculture, and technology, notably including James Watt's epoch-making invention and production of the steam engine.

Australian economic historian G.S.L. Tucker has argued that the investment of English savings in countries where wheat and other primary goods could be produced more cheaply than at home tended to raise and maintain the rate of profit and thereby enlarge the sphere of investment (Tucker 1960, p. 135). A declining rate of profit, by contrast, could neither be averted by investing in one form of manufacture instead of another, nor by transferring capital to agriculture rather than industry. Instead, for proponents of colonialism, the rate of profit could only be maintained and extended by exporting capital and labor to the colonies, "where they would produce the food and raw materials that England required, and at the same time create new and growing markets for her export industries." In so doing, Britain would no longer be so dependent on foreign markets and the exigencies of foreign tariff policies. Rather, by setting up a "colonial Zollverein" (or customs union) it would be able to control its own economic destiny (ibid, p. 141).

Despite being a staunch opponent of North American slavery, Liberal economist and political theorist John Stuart Mill was firmly convinced of the benefits of colonialism to human progress, so much so that he vouchsafed the option of the enslavement of colonized peoples. For Mill, whose advocacy of a liberal pluralist voting system based on the educational standards of citizens was explicitly formulated so as to exclude the representation of the broad working class (he feared that its numerical preponderance would lead to political domination), freedom applied "only to human beings in the maturity of their faculties" and could not be demanded by minors or "those backward states of society in which the race itself may be considered as in its nonage" (Mill 1972, p. 72). In Mill's view, "a ruler full of the spirit of improvement is warranted in the use of any expedients that will attain an end, perhaps otherwise unattainable" (ibid, p. 73). He demanded the barbarians' "obedience" for the purposes of their education for "continuous labor," the supposed foundation of civilization. In this context, writes Italian historian Domenico Losurdo (2011, pp. 225–6), Mill did not hesitate to theorize a transitional phase of "slavery" for "uncivilized races" (Mill 1972, p. 198), since there were "savage tribes so averse from regular industry, that industrial life is scarcely able to introduce itself among them until they are ... conquered and made slaves of" (Mill 1963–91, p. 247).

Mill was sanguine about the benefits of colonialism to the British economy:

"It is to the emigration of English capital, that we have chiefly to look for keeping up a supply of cheap food and cheap materials of clothing, proportional to the increase of our population; thus enabling an increasing capital to find employment in the country, without reduction of profit, in producing manufactured articles with which to pay for this supply of raw produce. Thus, the exportation of capital is an agent of great efficacy in extending the field of employment for that which remains: and it may be said truly that, up to a certain point, the more capital we send away, the more we shall possess and be able to retain at home" (Mill 1909, p. 739, quoted in Tucker, 1960, p. 136).

INTRODUCTION

For Porter (1984, p. 142), the centrality of the developing world to British capital accumulation was threefold:

"Firstly: in so far as it was developing, and not merely stagnant, it followed that it required more capital than it could provide itself: and this Britain could supply. In the 1890s, ninety-two per cent of the new capital Britain invested abroad went outside Europe, and half of it to the developing countries of Africa, Asia and Australasia. Secondly: from the commercial point of view it was a market which overall bought more from Britain than it sold—just; and such markets were becoming very rare. Thirdly: it was a market which, in so far as it had not been cornered by European rivals and surrounded by their tariffs or saturated with their capital, was still 'open.' 'Open' markets were getting hard to find in the protectionist 'nineties; but if Britain's products were to be sold abroad at all, those that were still open had to be kept open."

Economic historian Phyllis Deane lists six main ways that foreign trade contributed to catalysing what she calls the first industrial revolution. First, foreign trade created a demand for the products of British industry. Second, it provided access to raw materials which widened the range and cheapened the products of British industry. Third, international trade provided underdeveloped countries with the purchasing power to buy British goods. Fourth, it provided an economic surplus which helped finance industrial expansion and agricultural improvement, with the profits of trade having "overflowed into agriculture, mining and manufacture." Fifth, international trade helped to create an institutional structure and business ethic which was almost as effective in promoting the home trade as for the foreign trade. Finally, the expansion of international trade in the eighteenth century was a prime cause of the growth of large towns and industrial centres such as Liverpool and Glasgow (Deane 1965, pp. 66–68, quoted in Frank 1978, p. 227).

Capital Gains from Empire

What was the extent to which capitalism relied on colonialism for its advancement? We will examine several measures here, concentrating in particular on the British case. We encourage readers to research the impact of colonialism on other European economies. Our view is that an important reason why the shift in Europe in the exercise of state power from repression to inclusion could take place within a dynamic capitalist environment is due to the fruits of the colonial Empire. These came partly in the form of (1) imported colonial mass consumption goods, (2) raw materials imports for expanding British industry, (3) profit from colonial trade, taxes, and investments, and (4) an area for settlements for the "industrial reserve army"—the unemployed surplus population in Europe.

Hidden Colonial Surplus Value

Marxist author, teacher, activist, and a founding member of the Non-European Unity Movement in South Africa, his country of birth, Hosea Jaffe (1921–2014) coined the term "hidden colonial surplus value" to describe the large amount of surplus value transferred to the imperialist countries by the oppressed countries of Africa, Asia, and South America. This "hidden surplus value" is the difference between the selling price of Third World exports and the selling price of these same exports in the imperialist markets (Jaffe 1980, p. 113). The source of this cheapness is not purely "economic," but intrinsically a matter of political economy, that is, the ensemble of power relations within which goods and services are produced, distributed, and consumed.

For Jaffe, as for Cope (2015, p. 219), imperialist value transfers may be resolved into two components: repatriated profits and hidden surplus value. Repatriated profits represent only the visible portion of the value transfers generated by foreign investment and loan capital, whilst superprofits (the extra or above average surplus-value extracted from the labor of nationally oppressed workers) represent the invisible portions retrieved through capital export imperialism, unequal exchange, and debt usury.

As Jaffe has argued, and Cope (2015) has demonstrated applies in today's world economy, the intra-imperialist rate of profit may be negative if hidden surplus-value from invisible net transfers amounts to more than net profits. In such a case, value-added ($s + v$) is less than wages (v), and profits derive only from the exploited nations whilst wages are subsidized by superprofits. In short, were the Third World workers involved in the production of commodities for First World markets suddenly to be remunerated at the same rate as "workers" in the latter, the entirety of profits of the world's leading capitalist powers would be completely annihilated.

Jaffe estimates that no less than 500 million people were killed by Europeans during the four centuries of its primary accumulation of capital in the Americas, Asia, and Africa, an average of 100 million people per century at a time when the total world population increased from 300 million to 1 billion. As he writes: "This

400-year long process left a permanent mark on the value of human labor power of the colonial workers and on the immediate 'value' equivalent, in gold and its money representation, of the labor time of these workers" (ibid, p. 102).

Between the 16th and 19th centuries, the major international motors for European capital accumulation were the trade in African slaves carried in British and French ships; silver and gold exports from South America to Spain and Portugal; profits from the use of slave labor in the British West Indies; profits from the Dutch spice trade; profits from the opium trade; and colonial land revenue. In each case, colonialism as the expansion and acquisition of control of overseas territories by burgeoning capitalist European powers, many featuring unmitigated slavery, provided the impetus for nascent capitalist accumulation (Blaut 1980, p. 105).

Jaffe argues that during the first half of the 19th century, the wages of British, French, Dutch, and German workers differed little from the maintenance cost of slaves in the United States, Brazil, Cape, and the Dutch and French colonies. The rate of exploitation for these two distinct groups of workers (those from oppressed nations and those from oppressor nations) was more or less equally miserable. However, with the transition to imperialism in the second half of the 19th century, the ratio s/v rose for colonial and fell for metropolitan workers (ibid, p. 111).

INTRODUCTION

The Drain Theory of British Colonialism

Among the earliest writers to systematically analyse and oppose the parasitic relationship obtaining between a colonial and a colonising country was Parsi intellectual, teacher, cotton trader, and early Indian nationalist Dadhabai Naoroji (1825–1917). Naoroji, India's "grand old man," was the first Asian to be a member of the British Parliament (the House of Commons), which he was from 1892 to 1895. Naoroji formed the Indian National Congress together with A.O. Hume and Dinshaw Edulji Wacha. His book *Poverty and Un-British Rule in India* drew attention to England's exploitation of the country. One of the few contemporary descriptions of England's colonial exploitation comes from Naoroji. In an appeal from 1882, *On Justice for India*, addressed to the British parliament, and based on extensive statistical calculations of the transfer of wealth from India to Britain, Naoroji described how taxes, trading profits, the destruction of India's handicraft sector, and monopoly prices on imports from England to India drained the country. In 1896, the Indian National Congress officially adopted Naorojii's "drain theory" as their political criticism of colonialism. Naoroji considered that by dint of its oppressed position, India was subject to British capitalist exploitation without being thereby enabled to reap any of the fruits of capitalist development.

For Naoroji, there were several underlying bases for this unrecompensed transfer of India's wealth to Britain. First, he argued, India is a vast country ruled by a handful of Europeans whose income is a "moral drain," that is, a cost to British India. Second, India develops as a market for British manufactures and

Table I. India's Annual Balance of Payments of Current Account, 1869–73 to 1894–98 (£ millions, quinquennial average)

	Balance Merchandise Trade	Net Treasury Imports	Balance Visible Trade (1+2)	Home Charges	Other Invisible	All Invisibles (4+5)	Balance of Payments Current Account (3+6)
	1	2	3	4	5	6	7
1869–73	+22.6	-8.4	+14.2	-8.8	-15.6	-24.4	-10.2
1874–78	+21.0	-6.4	+14.6	-9.3	-18.0	-27.3	-12.7
1879–83	+23.8	-7.1	+16.7	-10.7	-17.7	-28.4	-11.7
1884–88	+23.8	-9.2	+14.6	-12.3	-18.0	-30.3	-15.7
1889–93	+25.2	-9.7	+15.5	-13.5	-19.4	-32.9	-17.4
1894–98	+20.7	-5.6	+15.1	-13.9	-18.9	-32.8	-17.7

Source: Banerji, 1982, Tables 34A and 40A in Karmakar, 2001, p. 70.

a supplier to Britain of its raw materials strictly because India's economic policies are dictated by Britain and in the interests of the British economy and the British capitalist class. Third, the Indian government under British rule is forced to pay an ever increasing list of official overseas expenses which Naoroji calls Home Charges (see Table 1). Fourth, rather than creating domestic employment and income, India's public expenditure out of the proceeds of taxation is instead used to pay for the infrastructure required by Britain to more effectively plunder the country. Finally, India's transformation into a "mere agrarian appendage and a subordinate trading partner" of Britain ensures that it has become a typical colony dominated from afar (Karmakar 2001, p. 69).

For Naoroji, the introduction of commercial relations in agriculture, capital investment in crop production, the imposition of a rural tax in kind, and the consequent monetisation of the Indian economy were not conducted on the basis of a thorough extirpation of the system of landlordism and a redistribution of landholdings amongst the peasantry, as in autochthonous capitalism, but on the incorporation of the landed class into a system of cash crop export dependency dominated by foreign capital. As such, Naoroji's "drain theory" was a precursor to Marxist theories of the "development of underdevelopment" (Andre Gunder Frank) and semi-feudalism.

The transfer of capital from India to Britain effected by colonial subordination precluded India from implementing development opportunities in the form of infrastructural investment, education, and so on. This view was later echoed by United States Marxist economist Paul Baran (1957, p. 163) who, having estimated that around 10 per cent of India's national product was transferred

Table II. Selected Data on the British Economy, 1830–1920

	Household consumption, £mn	Gross fixed capital formation (GFCF), £mn	Gov't consumption, £mn	Net trade, £mn	GDP at market prices, Expenditure side measure, £mn	GFCF as % of GDP
1830	448	25	31	-3	501	4.99
1840	490	55	33	-9	566	9.72
1850	508	47	38	2	593	7.93
1860	715	59	51	4	828	7.13
1870	954	87	55	17	1,153	7.55
1880	1,146	107	70	-29	1,379	7.76
1890	1,253	106	85	9	1,468	7.22
1900	1,637	205	182	-78	1,922	10.67
1910	1,877	158	182	1	2,216	7.13
1920	5,246	578	520	112	6,356	9.09

Source: Mitchell, chapter XVI, Table 5, pp. 831–35 in Bank of England, 2014.

to Britain each year in the early decades of the 20th century, wrote that "[far] from serving as an engine of economic expansion, of technological progress, and of social change, the capitalist order in these [underdeveloped] countries has represented a framework for economic stagnation, for archaic technology, and for social backwardness."

Nauroji estimated that Britain exacted an annual "tribute" from India of huge proportions. Following the Mutiny of 1857, India's First War of Independence, he estimated that the annual transfer from India to Great Britain amounted to a total of £30 million (Karmakar 2001, p. 67). Accepting Bank of England data (see Table II), we can say that between one third and one half of Britain's gross fixed capital formation (that is, the value of acquisitions of new or existing fixed assets by the business sector, governments, and households—excluding their unincorporated enterprises—less disposals of fixed assets and typically including land improvements; plant, machinery, and equipment purchases; and the construction of roads, railways, and the like, including schools, offices, hospitals, private residential dwellings, and commercial and industrial buildings), with the attendant productivity gain of British labor, was financed exclusively through the drain of India's wealth from colonial tribute.

British Income in the Absence of Empire

American economist Michael Edelstein specialising, inter alia, in the economics of the British Empire in the 19th century, has attempted to measure what Britain gained from the underdeveloped parts of its Empire. He has done so through positing a counterfactual condition, namely, that the aforementioned countries had remained independent.

Edelstein argues that if the Empire territories had remained independent of British rule they would not have participated in the international economy to the same extent that they, in fact, did. Thus, he writes, the British Raj brought a more peaceful, unified, and commercially oriented political economy to India than would have been the case if the country had remained independent. While we might argue that India was by no stretch of the imagination a peaceful place under British rule, or that it may have been more commercially engaged outside it than Edelstein supposes, his working assumption that Britain's trade with India and the other non-Dominion regions would have been a quarter of its existing level in 1870 and 1913 in the absence of British rule (Edelstein 1994, p. 203) is plausible.

What, then, is Edelstein's assessment of the gains made by Britain from trade with its oppressed colonies?

"Summing the 75 per cent reduction to British exports to the non-Dominion colonies and the 30 per cent reduction to British exports in the Dominion regions (weighted by their respective shares in British colonial exports), British colonial exports in 1870 and 1913 would have been 45 per cent of their actual levels under this 'strong non-imperialist' standard of the gains from Empire. (The shares of white-settler and non-white-settler colonies in British exports to the colonies were approximately 45 per cent and 55 per cent, respectively. With their 'strong' non-Empire levels hypothetically reduced to 0.7 and 0.25, respectively, of their actual levels, British exports to both types of colonies would have been = 45 per cent (0.7) + 55 per cent (0.25) = 45.25 per cent of actual levels.)

"The 'strong' gain is the difference between the actual British Empire exports and this hypothetical 45 per cent level in the absence of Empire. British exports of goods and services to the Empire were approximately 7.9 per cent and 11.9 per cent of GNP in 1870 and 1913; therefore the 'strong' gain from Empire was 4.3 per cent (i.e. 55 per cent of 7.9 per cent) of GNP in 1870 and 6.5 per cent of GNP in 1913" (Edelstein 1994, p. 204).

According to the Bank of England figures listed in Table II, gross fixed capital formation (GFCF) was 7.55 per cent of Britain's GDP in 1870 and 7.13 per cent of its GDP in 1910. Using Edelstein's "strong non-imperialist" standard, we may therefore suppose that around 57 per cent of Britain's fixed capital investment in 1870 ($4.3/7.5 \times 100$) and 91 per cent of its fixed capital investment in 1910 ($6.5/7.13 \times 100$) was funded by its trade with the colonies.

British–Indian Merchandise Trade and Capital Accumulation

Specifically colonial trade differs from domestic and other foreign trade. Crucially, the colonial market is kept compulsorily open while the metropolitan market is strictly protected; in the case of Britain against Asian textiles, for instance, draconian tariff duties were applied for 150 years. Moreover, as Indian Marxist economist Utsa Patnaik notes, "colonial goods for export were purchased out of local tax revenues raised from the colonized population as in India, or by the export-goods equivalent of slave rent as in the West Indies" (Patnaik 2006, p. 36). In effect, either the money paid to the colonial goods exporter by the colonial power came out of high taxes that the latter had itself paid to the colonial state, as in the case of India, or the export goods were the commodity form of economic surplus directly taken in the form of rent (slave rent as in the West Indies, and land rent as in Ireland). Finally, India's foreign exchange earnings were appropriated by Britain so as to settle its trade deficits with continental Europe and the USA (see below).

As shown in Table I, the nominal balance of trade includes more than direct merchandise trade, making it appear that Britain ran a trade surplus, not deficit, with its colonies. For no matter how great the trade surplus became (in 1913 India had the second largest trade surplus earnings in the world at £71 million), much larger fictitious invisible political charges were imposed to nullify the increased export earnings and, in fact, produce a small deficit on current account. Thus, as Patnaik highlights, countries with large and growing merchandise export surpluses such as India and Malaysia had more than their exports earnings siphoned off by Britain through politically imposed invisible burdens and had to borrow, while the country with a large and growing trade deficit, Britain, was able to siphon off the exchange earnings of its colonies and more than offset its current account deficit with sovereign regions, so that it actually exported capital to these regions on an increasing scale (Patnaik 2006, p. 41).

Nonetheless, as Patnaik shows, the unpaid trade surpluses extracted from the oppressed nations of the British Empire allowed

British capital accumulation to advance rapidly. By calculating the direct merchandise import surplus from India and the West Indies into Britain and using this as the measure of surplus transfer from these colonized regions, Patnaik (2006) estimates the level of Britain's rates of capital formation that were thereby made possible. She finds that the combined colonial transfer expressed as a percentage of Britain's savings, is at least 62.2 in 1770, 86.4 in 1801, 85.9 in 1811, and 65.9 in 1821 (Patnaik 2006, pp. 49–50, quoted in Cope, 2014, pp. 276–278).

Britain's capital accumulation was intimately connected to its plunder of the colonies. Value transferred from the Third World, over and above the prevailing domestic level, raises the profitability of First World business not only by cheapening the costs of constant and variable capital, allowing for much higher rates of consumption of both, but also, in the colonial era at least, by allowing for increased rates of capital formation through unpaid trade surpluses.

Colonialism, Popular Consumption, and Labor Reformism

It is clear from the above that European capitalists derived enormous wealth from colonialism. The British economy was in part the product of commercial hegemony achieved through imperialism, allowing Britain to become industrialized with a large proletarian population. However, the question remains: to what extent did the European proletariat itself benefit from colonialism? We argue here that despite creating much of the surplus value produced by their respective nations in the earlier part of the industrial capitalist era, the European proletariat between 1875 and 1950 (roughly the era of high imperialist colonialism) was nourished by colonized peoples' labor, their incomes were dependent on the proceeds of colonialism, and their employment was a function of the maintenance of colonialism. The divide between the workers of the colonial nations and those in the colonized nations widened as imperialism advanced so that both the living conditions and the political horizons of each group of workers became increasingly polarized. We will examine here how colonialism raised the living standards of all European workers, particularly those organized workers poised to exploit the scarcity of their skills, as well as their "racial" and religious affiliations, vis-à-vis the colonized.

Capital and revenues from the colonies made wage increases for the metropolitan working class possible. Wages in England increased relative to prices by 26 per cent in the 1870s, 21 per cent in the 1880s, and 11 per cent in the 1890s. It was skilled workers who particularly benefited. A skilled worker earned approximately twice that of an unskilled worker, still living just above subsistence level.

The working class had, following the political reforms of the second half of the 19th Century, organized into powerful trade unions. This allowed the upper layers of skilled workers to obtain better wages and working conditions as well as expansion of trade union rights. This wage increase—which occurred first in England and later in France, Germany, and other Western European countries—contributed to the expansion of consumption power and to the reduction of the recurring overproduction crises that capitalism had hitherto suffered.

The only way wage levels could rise without the profit rate falling below what was necessary for capital accumulation, was by the exploitation of an increasing number of people employed in the colonial areas as workers in plantations, mines, and factories. Here, wages were set at subsistence level or less. The superexploitation of labor was the basis of the higher profits for capital invested in the colonies. The fall in the rate of profit that would have occurred as a result of rising wages in Europe was thereby compensated for by the increasing amounts of surplus labor performed in the colonies. On the one hand, capital benefited from rising wages at home by raising effective demand for commodities, while on the other hand, the low wages in the colonial areas maintained high profits. In this way colonialism solved the contradiction of capitalism in the North by dissolving the stagnating effect of higher wages within the enhanced exploitation of the proletariat in the South.

Economist Joan Robinson (1970, pp. 64–6) described the link between colonialism, the development of capitalism in Europe, and working-class consumption patterns:

"It was not only superior productivity that caused capitalist wealth to grow. The whole world was ransacked for resources. The dominions overseas that European nations had been acquiring and fighting over since the sixteenth century and others also, were now greatly developed to supply raw materials to industry. ... The industrial workers at home gained from imperialism in three ways. First of all, raw materials and foodstuffs were cheap relatively to manufactures which maintained the purchasing power of their wages. Tea, for instance, from being a middle-class luxury became an indispensable necessity for the English poor. Secondly the great

Figure I. Index of real wages in England, 1850-1905

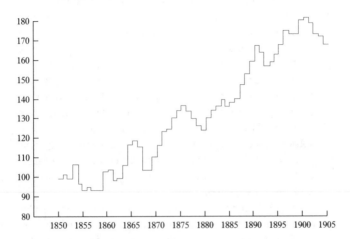

Source: Jones, 1974, p. 170.

fortunes made in industry, commerce and finance spilled over to the rest of the community in taxes and benefactions while continuing investment kept the demand for labor rising with the population. ... Finally, lording it around the world as members of the master nations, they could feed their self-esteem upon notions of racial superiority. ... Thus the industrial working class, while apparently struggling against the system, was in fact absorbed in it."

INTRODUCTION

Imperial Consumption

The most important commercial crop at the beginning of the 19th century was sugar. Produced by slave labor, its sale generated enormous profits for sugar merchants, plantation owners, and investors. Sugar consumption in Britain doubled between 1690 and 1740. By the 1830s and the advent of industrialised textile production, however, its market value had been exceeded by cotton. Britain was unable to produce cotton and imported all of it from America, where it was produced by slaves, and from Egypt and India, where it was produced by subsistence peasants. Raw cotton, sugar, rum, and tobacco imports were shipped by the tonne into prosperous British ports like Bristol, London, and Liverpool (see, for instance, Lane, 1987); all originated in the expanding slave plantations of America and the Caribbean.

Many of Britain's primary products were producible exclusively in colonized tropical countries, though some were "temperate" food grains from colonies such as Ireland and India, as well as from the settler-colonial United States. In 1800 and at the height of the industrial revolution, an estimated 18 per cent of beef and pork consumption, 11 per cent of butter and margarine consumption, and 12 per cent of wheat and wheaten flour consumption in Britain was met by Irish imports (Jones 1981, p. 67). British importing of Irish grain, cattle, butter and so on contributed to the hellish starvation in Ireland in the 1840s and 1850s, from which that country's population has still not recovered almost two centuries later. These temperate foodstuffs came to constitute 31 per cent of all imports of food and drink in 1844–6 and fully 43 per cent in

1854–6 (Davis 1979, p. 37). The most important items of direct mass consumption for which there was substantial or complete import dependence were wheat (of which India was probably the third most significant source) and wheaten flour, rice, cane sugar (beet sugar production in Continental Europe being fairly insignificant), tea, coffee, and tobacco. Of these, only the first was produced in Britain but production was not growing as fast as population between 1700 and 1850.

From the middle of the 19th century, a substantial general rise in incomes, particularly, as Davis notes, those of a large minority of the population (farmers, many kinds of skilled workers, the professional classes, and rentiers), led to a sudden leap in demand for semi-luxury food and drinks and a sharp increase in the amount consumed per head. In this period Britain shifted to "the kind of import dependence in which starvation, rather than inconvenience or even poverty, became the alternative to importing" (Davis 1979, p. 52).

Whereas standard long-run real wage series simply divide the nominal wage by the price of an unchanging consumption basket, Hersh and Voth (2009) show that after Europe's "discovery" of America, its consumption habits were profoundly transformed and dramatically improved. They calculate that income gains from colonial goods imports such as tea, coffee, and sugar added at least the equivalent of 16 per cent, and possibly as much as 20 per cent, of household income to British people's welfare by the middle of the 19th century. For McCants (2007, p. 436), the intercontinental luxury trades of the early modern period transformed the European economy. Moreover, it was not purely the consumption habits of

Europe's elites that drove this transformation, but those of its working and middle classes:

"Who was drinking all of this tea and coffee? Surely not just wealthy elites, as the volumes are too high to even entertain the possibility of limited social access to hot caffeinated beverages. Some of the import volume was 'lost' to re-exports, but the ultimate consumers of these re-exports were, of course, just other Europeans (or their colonial counterparts). Eighteenth century commentators of all national stripes did not hesitate to ascribe consumption of these caffeinated luxuries, usually as a complaint, to the teeming masses of their social inferiors. Probate inventory evidence on the social diffusion of the artefacts associated with this consumption has been accumulating over the past several decades, and it suggests that it was indeed widespread across the social landscape" (McCants 2007, p. 446).

Investigating the consumption habits of European nations over the course of two centuries, popular consumption historian Carol Shammas has defined an item of mass consumption as one consumed by over a quarter of the population, showing that tobacco passed the mass consumption threshold by the middle of the 17th century and sugar at the end of the 17th century (McCants 2007, p. 449).

The mass consumption of these and other consumer imports proceeded apace with the liberalisation of trade, the incorporation of new producer countries in the international market, and the decline of prices all predicated on the expansion of Empire. McCants (2007) summarizes the main trends:

"The consumption of tea, coffee, sugar, tobacco, porcelain, and silk and cotton textiles, increased dramatically in western Europe beginning as early as the closing decades of the seventeenth century, only to accelerate through much of the eighteenth century. The consumer setbacks associated with the period of the French Revolution and a continent at war, especially as triggered by the Napoleonic blockades, should properly be seen as a severe interruption to the trend which would otherwise have extended rather more seamlessly from the early modern trade system to the 'transport revolution' of the nineteenth century. Use of the new commodities brought by this trade spread rapidly, both in geographical and social space. ... [The] presence of many of these so-called luxury goods is well documented down into the ranks of the working poor by the middle of the eighteenth century. There can be little doubt then, that European demand was fuelled not only by the rich with their growing 'surplus incomes' but by the much more numerous lower and middling classes of Europe's multitude of urban centres, followed by their rural counterparts."

Over the course of the 1700s perhaps 11 million slaves were exported by European merchants from Africa to the slave colonies on the opposite side of the Atlantic to produce many of these luxury items or their raw materials. As many as one in five slaves died during the journey, after enduring cramped, filthy, and dangerous conditions. Many more would die later on the plantations as a result of disease, overwork, and maltreatment. The expansion of the transatlantic slave trade can be located in the growth of popular consumer demand, behind which lay the sale into bondage of many millions of Africans.

INTRODUCTION

The Political Consequences: From Revolution to Reform

There has been considerable research into the 19th century English labor aristocracy. Both contemporary political opinion and historical research agree that it was the upper layer of organized skilled workers who constituted the labor aristocracy, and that its size and importance changed with economic conditions in the second half of the 19th century. The crucial point is that colonialism and imperialism opened up the possibility of increasing welfare for the metropolitan working class within the framework of capitalism. Reformism became a successful political line and, in tandem, the revolutionary line subsided.

The new economic trends changed the conditions of class struggle. The economic and political improvements that the capitalist class could not provide in the first half of the century—because it was impossible within that regime of accumulation—began to be provided towards the end of the century. Ruling class largesse (such as it was) was definitely not offered voluntarily. But in the first half of the century wage rises and political enfranchisement of the proletariat was a life and death question for capital. Now it became possible for capital to accede to these demands. Higher wages, improved working conditions, and extended political rights strengthened the faith of the working class in reformism and made it ever safer for capitalists to give the working class more power. Revolution was no longer on the agenda in Western Europe.

Hobsbawm (1964, p. 341) observed the relationship between colonialism and the development of a strong reformist current within the working class, stating: "The further we progress into the imperialist era, the more difficult does it become to put one's finger on groups of workers which did not in one way or another draw advantage from Britain's position […]."

From Internationalism to Nationalism

Marx and Engels coined the battle cry: "Proletarians of all countries, unite!" in *The Communist Manifesto* in 1848, expressing their hope for working-class solidarity across national boundaries—and even between imperial powers and their colonies—in a common struggle for a socialist revolution. However, they became disillusioned with the prospects for the same. They pointed out several times the relationship between colonialism and Britain's position as an imperial power and the embourgeoisement of its working class, that is, the proliferation of middle-class living standards and ideologies amongst the workforce. This can be seen, for example, in Engels's letter to Marx dated October 7th, 1858 (page 90), Engels's letter to Kautsky dated September 12th, 1882 (page 123), or Engels's letter to Bebel dated August 30th, 1883 (page 125 of this book).

The labor movement in the imperialist countries had not only difficulties demonstrating solidarity with the people in the colonies; they had also difficulties coming to terms with oppressed ethnic groups or nations struggling for equal rights at "home." This issue is played out most clearly in the United States over the question of slavery. In England, the Irish immigrants' struggle for equal rights is a parallel. The Irish immigrants were seen as competitors to the English workers and were met with hostility. National chauvinism—the belief in national superiority—played a prominent role in the politics of the English working class. In a letter to Meyer and Vogt of April 9th, 1870 (page 108), Marx compares the British working-class attitude to colonial Ireland and the Irish working class with white Americans' attitude to slaves in the American South.

Marx and Engels's political practice in this period was centered on the First International Working Men's Association, which in reality consisted of trade unions and political organizations from the Northwestern part of Europe. The divergent wage levels between the imperial powers and the colonies, and between different ethnic groups within the imperial center, were already an important issue of the time as, for instance, between English and Irish workers in England and between German and Czech workers in Germany. In his speech to the Lausanne Congress of the First International in 1867, Marx ([1867] 1975, p. 422) declared:

"A study of the struggle waged by the English working class reveals that, in order to oppose their workers, the employers either bring in workers from abroad or else transfer manufacture to countries where there is a cheap labor force. Given this state of affairs, if the working class wishes to continue its struggle with some chance of success, the national organizations must become international."

Marx already had an eye for the significance of differences in national wage levels for the prospects of developing an international class struggle—and that at a time in history where the wage gap was much less stark than today. Marx's strategy in relation to this situation was clear: international solidarity and struggle. Instead, defense of imperialism would become cemented in the British working class in the years ahead.

Imperialist Reformism and the Labor Aristocracy

In Victorian England, we see precisely the kind of social imperialism *avant la lettre* of which the Western left would find itself approving as superprofits increased:

"The domestic Radical programme, like the Fabian program of a few years later, rested on the assumption that home and foreign affairs had in practice very little connection. At home, the task of the radicals was to promote a more even distribution of wealth; but the wealth that was to be redistributed was taken for granted, without any examination of its sources. It was regarded, in effect, as natural and assured that Great Britain, as the leader of world industrialism, should go on getting richer and richer, and should devote her surplus capital resources to the exploitation of the less developed regions of the world, drawing therefrom an increasing tribute which Radical legislation would proceed to redistribute by means of taxation more equitably between the rich and the poor in Great Britain" (Cole and Postgate 1949, pp. 411–412).

According to Kirk (1985, p. 9), the ranks of the labor aristocracy were broadened in the second half of the 19th century with the rapid expansion of the capital goods sector and its high demand for skilled males, new labor aristocrats in the metal trades joining older ones in building and printing in the capitals of England and Scotland. The political moderation of the mid-Victorian labor movement, especially its trade union component, was due largely to the increased dominance of these skilled males therein, and its having laid in the hands of "moderate and 'responsible' men who, whilst laying strong claims to the rights of male citizenship, wished to achieve a stake in society" (ibid, p. 11).

At least in terms of the third quarter of the 19th century, Kirk argues that Hobsbawm is correct to draw a close connection between the "distinct if modest" improvement in all but the environmental conditions of the working class and increased political moderation. The evidence points to a clear rise in the living standards of a significant section of the British working class from around 1860 and an increasing differential between many skilled and lesser- and unskilled male workers during that period (McClelland 2000, p. 104).

With some important qualifications and corrections, it is valid to posit "an overall link between economic improvement and reformism during the third quarter of the century" (Kirk 1985, p. 81). Thus cotton operatives were generally much better off in material terms in 1875 than they had been in 1850, with the post-1864 years being a period of substantial, indeed, in many cases, spectacular rises in money and real incomes. Given this overall improvement, Kirk argues, "it is surely not coincidental that reformism took increasingly deep root in the cotton towns" (ibid, p. 82). Certainly many labor leaders consciously attributed their newfound moderation to the material and institutional gains of the years after 1850. That there had been real improvements in the standard of living of the working class was explicitly vouched for in the analysis of working-class reformers and their allies at the time (see, for example, Ludlow and Jones, 1867).

Alongside structural changes in the capitalist mode of production (Stedman Jones 1975), rising living standards brought about by falling prices, and the ability of trade union organisations to ensure that wages did not fall concurrently (of which more below), Kirk accounts for working-class conservatism by highlighting conflicts following a massive and unprecedented increase in the level of Irish Roman Catholic immigration into the cotton districts. In the years after the catastrophic famine of the late 1840s, this led to tensions between sections of the immigrant and host communities. Kirk establishes that a "working class fragmented [we would emphasize, stratified—ZC and TL] along ethnic (and wider cultural) lines greatly facilitated the (re)-assertion of bourgeois control upon the working class, and helped to attach workers more firmly to the framework of bourgeois politics" (Kirk 1985, p. 310). Thus, "[ethnic] conflict operated, against the background of the apparent inevitability of capitalism, to restrict further the potential for class solidarity in Lancashire and Cheshire, and to provide sections of the bourgeoisie with the opportunity to assert their authority, in a fairly direct way, upon workers" (ibid, p. 335).

Stedman Jones (1971, pp. 241–2) argues that the extension of the franchise to part of the male working class in Britain with the Reform Act of 1867 (the Second Reform Act) was the means employed by the ruling class to forestall "an incipient alliance between the casual 'residuum' and the 'respectable working class,' as fear grew on a national level of a possible coalition between reformers, trade unions and the Irish." Indeed, this analysis is borne out with the example of fiscal policy with respect to sugar duties:

"Government strategy was driven by a number of different elements, not least the fiscal problems of the state. It was necessary to increase revenues by imposing income tax, beginning to shift the burden of taxation from indirect to direct taxes and, at the same time, keeping income tax low through increasing revenues by lowering duties on consumption goods and thus boosting, in particular, working-class consumption. This has to be seen in the broader context of, on the one hand, dealing with the Chartist insurgency by attempting to attach the working class to the state through encouraging consumption and some measures of social reform and, on the other, of dealing with the interests of manufacturing and the effects of the economic depression of 1837–42 through attacking the Corn Law problem. The latter would also entail addressing the crisis in Ireland by moving towards free trade as the putative solution.

"Within the wider framework, [British Conservative Chancellor of the Exchequer and slave plantation owner Henry] Goulburn situated his aims so far as sugar was concerned. Sugar had become an essential element of working-class consumption so his aim was 'to secure to the people of this country an ample supply of sugar.' But he also wished to make that supply 'consistent with a continued resistance to the Slave Trade, and with the encouragement of the abolition of slavery.' Finally, he sought 'to reconcile both with a due consideration to the interests of those who have vested their property in our Colonial possessions.'" (Hall et al 2014, p. 145)

However militant the labor aristocracy's struggles against employers over the past century (and these are frequently and massively exaggerated), they were never directed against the division between oppressor and oppressed nations, against the imperialist system that guaranteed the amount of colonial loot to be divided amongst the warring parties.

Imperial Trade Unionism

The bargaining power of metropolitan wage labor improved as the outmigration of the unemployed to settler and non-settler colonies reduced the size of the reserve army of labor, and as the huge inflow of colonial transfers boosted domestically generated productivity, profits, and investment, thus serving to raise mass living standards.

The connection between labor reformism and colonialism was, however, even more direct. As primary wealth-creators, the major producer industries of the Victorian period were agriculture, textiles, coal, iron and steel, and engineering. These industries were also the major employers, the major export earners and, in the latter part of the century, the major targets for the newly emerging trades unions. In 1889 trades unions had 679,000 members, the majority of whom were in the primary industries. By 1900 there were over two million union members in Britain. Of equal importance was the diversification of industry in this period, along with the ever-increasing range of imported products. According to data compiled by Clegg et al (1964), the majority of the unionized workers in the late 19th century were in iron and steel, coal mining, and cotton and woollen textiles.

Clough (1993) explains how the economic and political benefits accruing to the skilled working class of Victorian England organized in these industries were directly attributable to their exceptional position in the international division of labor at the time, that is, to British colonial imperialism:

"If we look at the sectors where skilled workers and their

Table III. Trade Union Membership in Britain, 1888 and 1892

	1888		1892	
	Union Membership (1000s)	Union Density (%)	Union Membership (1000s)	Union Density (%)
Metals, engineering & shipbuilding	190	19.5	310.2	31.9
Mining & quarrying	150	24.2	326.7	52.6
Textiles	120	10.5	203.1	17.7
Great Britain	750	6.2	1,576.0	13.0

Source: Hatton et al, 1994. Union membership data for 1888 are from Clegg et al, 1964, p. 1. Membership data for 1892 are from Bain and Price, 1980. The union densities were calculated using industry employment data for 1891 from Bain and Price, 1980.

organisation were strongest, we find them to be closely connected to Empire: textiles, iron and steel, engineering, and coal. Textiles because of the cheap cotton from Egypt, and a captive market in India; iron and steel because of ship-building and railway exports, engineering because of the imperialist arms industry, and coal because of the demands of Britain's monopoly of world shipping. In a myriad of different ways, the conditions of the labor aristocracy were bound up with the maintenance of British imperialism. And this fact was bound to be reflected in their political standpoint."

Meanwhile, Hatton et al (1994) have found that the effect of union membership on earnings at this time was of the order of 15–20% and that this effect was similar at different skill levels. A broadly similar pattern is observed for industry groups, although the difference in the impact of unions on earnings across industries was greater than across skill groups.

Socialist Internationalism and Anti-Imperialism Today

Since decolonisation, there has been a shift from value transfer based on colonial tribute to that based on imperialist rent, that is, "the above average or extra profits realized as a result of the inequality between North and South in the global capitalist system" dominated by Western monopolies (Higginbottom 2014, p. 24). The mass embourgeoisement of the metropolitan working classes via receipt of value transferred from the exploited nations and minority communities and the attendant political pacification is not admitted by socialists in the imperialist countries. The point to be grasped by the genuine left—those struggling to see an end to capitalism and imperialism alike—is that so long as imperialism functions, internationalist labor movements in the core imperialist countries will be strictly delimited.

INTRODUCTION

In *The Eighteenth Brumaire of Louis Bonaparte*, Marx remarked that "[t]he Roman proletariat lived at the expense of society, while modern society lives at the expense of the proletariat" since almost all of Rome's wealth derived from landlordism, slavery, and imperial tribute. The Roman proletariat (from the Latin *proles*, "offspring") had little in common with the proletariat of capitalist society. It was considered useful for little but siring children to serve as soldiers or settlers for the empire. As such, the proletariat was a parasitic class that was maintained at the expense of the empire's peasants, slaves, and colonized peoples. In that sense, it was much like the First World working class of today, which is largely maintained by the surplus labor of proletarians, peasants, and slaves in the exploited nations.

Fighting for higher wages and better living conditions for First World workers is reactionary outside of the struggle against imperialism. Government deficit spending, expanded welfare measures, and protected industry in the affluent countries are not necessarily socialist measures. Those groups, whether ostensibly left-wing or right-wing, which act to preserve the inequality of imperialist relations invariably promote national chauvinist solutions to problems of unemployment and declining living standards (Baran 1978, p. 247). The increasingly respectable fascist movement promises the highest levels of parasitism for white workers, national business interests unhappy with neo-liberalism, and the petty-bourgeoisie opposed to the fiscal requirements of globalized finance capital. The denial of gigantic imperialist value transfer adds fuel to the fire of right-wing populism.

Bibliography:

Acemoglu, Daron, Simon Johnson, and James Robinson. 2002. *The Rise of Europe: Atlantic Trade, Institutional Change and Economic Growth*. Berkeley, November 25. Online: http://scholar.harvard.edu/files/jrobinson/files/jr_AERAtlanticTrade.pdf

Bain, G.S. and R. Price. 1980. *Profiles of Union Growth: A Comparative Statistical Portrait of Eight Countries*. Oxford: Basil Blackwell.

Banerji, A.K. 1982. *Aspects of Indo-British Economic Relations, 1858–1898*. Oxford: Oxford University Press.

Bank of England. 2014. "Three centuries of macroeconomic data." Online: http://www.bankofengland.co.uk/research/Pages/onebank/threecenturies.aspx

Baran, Paul. 1957. *The Political Economy of Growth*. New York: Monthly Review Press.

Bhattacharya, Sabyasachi. 2006. "International Flows of Un-free Labour." In Jomo K.S., editor, *Globalization under Hegemony: The Changing World Economy*. Delhi: Oxford University Press, 195–227

Blaut, James M. 1987. *The National Question: Decolonizing the Theory of Nationalism*. London: Zed Press.

———— 1993. *The Colonizer's Model of the World: Geographical Diffusionism and Eurocentric History.* New York: Guilford Press.

Bleaney, Michael. 1976, *Underconsumption Theories: A History and Critical Analysis.* London: Lawrence and Wishart.

Clegg, H.A., Alan Fox, and A.F. Thompson. 1964. *A History of British Trade Unions Since 1889,* vol. 1. Oxford: Oxford University Press.

Clough, Robert. 1993. "Haunted by the labour aristocracy. Part 1: Marx and Engels on the split in the working class." In *Fight Racism! Fight Imperialism!,* no. 115, October/November.

Cole, G.D.H. and Raymond Postgate. 1949. *The Common People, 1746–1946.* London: Methuen and Co. Ltd.

Cope, Zak. 2014. "Final Comments on Charles Post's Critique of the Theory of the Labour Aristocracy." In Paul Zarembka, editor, *Sraffa and Althusser Reconsidered; Neoliberalism Advancing in South Africa, England, and Greece* (Research in Political Economy, Volume 29). Emerald Group Publishing Limited, 275–286.

———— 2015. *Divided World Divided Class: Global Political Economy and the Stratification of Labour under Capitalism.* Second edition. Montreal, Quebec: Kersplebedeb.

Cottrell, P.L. [1980] 2006. *Industrial Finance, 1830–1914: The Finance and Organization of the English Manufacturing Industry.* London: Routledge.

Davis, Mike. 2000. "The Origin of the Third World." *Antipode*, vol. 32, no. 1, 48–89.

Davis, Ralph. 1979. *The Industrial Revolution and British Overseas Trade*. Leicester: Leicester University Press.

Deane, Phyllis. 1965. *The First Industrial Revolution*. Cambridge: Cambridge University Press.

Edelstein, Michael. 1994. "Imperialism: cost and benefit." In Roderick Floud and Donald McCloskey, editors, *The Economic History of Britain since 1700. Volume 2: 1860–1939*. Second edition. Cambridge: Cambridge University Press, 197–217.

Engels, Frederick. [1880] 1970. "Socialism: Utopian and Scientific." In *Marx and Engels: Selected Works*. Moscow: Progress Publishers.

——— [1848] 1976. "The Movements of 1847." In *Marx-Engels Collected Works*, vol. 6. Moscow: Progress Publishers.

Field, John. 1978. "British historians and the concept of the labor aristocracy." *Radical History Review*, no. 19, 61–85.

Frank, Andre Gunder. 1978. *World Accumulation, 1492–1789*. London: Macmillan Press.

Gallagher, John and Ronald Robinson. 1953. "The Imperialism of Free Trade." In *Economic History Review*, vol. 6, no. 1.

Habib, Irfan. 2002. *Essays in Indian History: Towards a Marxist Perception*. London: Anthem Press.

Hall, Catherine, Keith McClelland, Nick Draper, Kate Donington, and Rachel Lang. 2014. *Legacies of British Slave-Ownership: Colonial Slavery and the Formation of Victorian Britain*. Cambridge: Cambridge University Press.

Hatton, T.J., G.R. Boyer, and R.E. Bailey. 1994. "The union wage effect in late nineteenth century Britain." Online: http://digitalcommons.ilr.cornell.edu/articles/537/

Hersh, Jonathan and Hans-Joachim Voth. 2009. "Sweet Diversity: Colonial Goods and the Rise of European Living Standards after 1492." July 17. Online: http://ssrn.com/abstract=1402322 or http://dx.doi.org/10.2139/ssrn.1402322

Higginbottom, Andy. 2014. "'Imperialist Rent' in Practice and Theory." In *Globalizations*, vol. 11, no. 1. Special Issue: Free Trade and Transnational Labour, 23–33.

Hobsbawm, Eric J. 1957. "The British Standard of Living 1790–1850." In *The Economic History Review*, vol. 10, no. 1, 46–68.

Jaffe, Hosea. 1980. *The Pyramid of Nations*. Milan: Victor.

Jones, E.L. 1981. "Agriculture, 1700–1800." In Roderick Floud and Donald McCloskey, editors, *The Economic History of Britain Since 1700. Volume I, 1700–1860*. Cambridge: Cambridge University Press.

Jones, Gareth Stedman. 1971. *Outcast London: A Study in the Relationship between Classes in Victorian Society*. Oxford: Oxford University Press.

———— 1975. "Class Struggle and the Industrial Revolution." *New Left Review*, vol. 90.

Jones, Richard Benjamin. 1974. *Economic and Social History of England, 1770–1970*. London: Longman.

Karmakar, Asim K. 2001. "Dadhabai Naoroji, Drain Theory and Poverty: Towards a Discourse in Political Economy." In P.D. Hajela, editor, *Economic Thoughts of Dadabhai Naoroji*. New Delhi: Deep and Deep Publications.

Kelly, M.G.E. 2015. *Biopolitical Imperialism*. Winchester, UK: Zero Books.

Kennedy, Paul. 1987. *The Rise and Fall of the Great Powers: Economic Change and Military Conflict from 1500 to 2000*. New York: Random House.

Kittrell, Edward R. 1965. "The Development of the Theory of Colonization in English Classical Political Economy." First published in *Southern Economic Journal*. Volume XXXI. In A.G.L. Shaw, editor. 1970. *Great Britain and the Colonies, 1815–1865*. London: Methuen & Co Ltd.

Kirk, Neville. 1985. *The Growth of Working-Class Reformism in Mid-Victorian England*. London: Croom Helm.

Krooth, Richard. 2015. "Imperialism and the Sources of Surplus Value." In Immanuel Ness and Zak Cope, editors, *Palgrave Encyclopedia of Imperialism and Anti-Imperialism*. New York: Palgrave Macmillan.

Kuhn, Gabriel. 2014. *Turning Money into Rebellion: The Unlikely Story of Denmark's Revolutionary Bank Robbers*. Oakland, California and Montreal, Quebec: PM Press and Kersplebedeb.

Lane, Tony. 1987. *Liverpool: Gateway of Empire*. London: Lawrence and Wishart Ltd.

Lauesen, Torkil and Zak Cope. 2015. "Imperialism and the Transformation of Values into Prices." *Monthly Review*. Volume 67, Issue 3, July.

Losurdo, Domenico. 2011. *Liberalism: A Counter-History*. London: Verso.

Ludlow, J.M. and Lloyd Jones. 1867. *The Progress of the Working Class, 1832–1867*. London: Alexander Strahan.

MacDonagh, Oliver. 1962. "The Anti-Imperialism of Free Trade." In *Economic History Review*, vol. 14, no. 3.

Marx, Karl. [1867] 1954. *Capital*. Volume I. Moscow: Foreign Languages Publishing House.

Marx, Karl and Friedrich Engels. [1867] 1975. "Congress of the International Workingmen's Association in Lausanne." In *Collected Works*, vol. 20, p. 422. New York: International Publishers.

McCants, Anne E.C. 2007. "Exotic Goods, Popular Consumption, and the Standard of Living: Thinking About Globalization in the Early Modern World." *Journal of World History*, vol. 18, no. 4, 433–62.

McClelland, Keith. 2000. "'England's Greatness, the Working Man'." In Catherine Hall, Keith McClelland, and Jane Rendall, editors, *Defining the Victorian Nation: Race, Gender and the British Reform Act of 1867*. Cambridge: Cambridge University Press, 71–119.

Mill, John Stuart. [1848, 7th edition 1871] 1909. *Principles of Political Economy*. London: W.J. Ashley.

——— 1963–91. *Collected Works*, Volume 2. Edited by John M. Robson, Toronto and London: University of Toronto Press and Routledge and Kegan Paul.

——— [1861] 1972. *Utilitarianism, Liberty, Representative Government*. Edited by Harry B. Acton. London: Dent.

Mitchell, B.R. 1988. *British Historical Statistics*. Cambridge University Press.

Morris, R.J. 1988. "The Labour Aristocracy in the British Class Struggle." *ReFRESH*, no.7, Autumn. Online: http://www.ehs.org.uk/dotAsset/aa433527-7c66-425a-8cbf-cc590e4bd083.pdf

Nehru, Jawaharlal. [1934] 1982. *Glimpses of World History*. Delhi: Oxford University Press.

Patnaik, Utsa. 2006. "The free lunch: transfers from the tropical colonies and their role in capital formation in Britain during the industrial revolution." In Jomo K.S., editor, *Globalisation under hegemony: the changing world economy*. Oxford: Oxford University Press, 37–71.

BIBLIOGRAPHY

Porter, Bernard. 1984. *The Lion's Share: A Short History of British Imperialism, 1850–1983.* London: Longman.

Robinson, Joan. 1970. *Freedom and Necessity: An Introduction to the Study of Society.* London: George Allen and Unwin.

Rothstein, Theodore. 1983 [1929]. *From Chartism to Labourism: Historical Sketches of the English Working Class Movement.* London: Lawrence and Wishart.

Shammas, Carole. 1990. *The Pre-industrial Consumer in England and America.* Oxford University Press.

Sweezy, Paul. 1949. *The Theory of Capitalist Development: Principles of Marxian Political Economy.* London: Dennis Dobson Ltd.

Thomas, R.P. and D.N. McCloskey. 1981. "Overseas Trade and Empire, 1700–1860." In Roderick Floud and Donald McCloskey, editors, *The Economic History of Britain Since 1700*, Volume I, 1700–1860. Cambridge: Cambridge University Press.

Tucker, G.S.L. 1960. "The Application and Significance of Theories of the Effect of Economic Progress on the Rate of Profit, 1800-1850." In A.G.L. Shaw, editor. 1970. *Great Britain and the Colonies, 1815–1865.* London: Methuen & Co Ltd.

Williams, Eric. 1944. *Capitalism and Slavery.* North Carolina: University of North Carolina Press.

Abbreviations:

MESW Karl Marx and Friedrich Engels: *Selected Works*, Vol. 1–2 (Foreign Languages Publishing House, Moscow) 1951.

KMC Karl Marx: *Capital*, Vol. I–III (Foreign Languages Publishing House, Moscow) 1962.

MESC Karl Marx and Friedrich Engels: *Selected Correspondence* (Progress Publishers, Moscow) 1965.

MEOC Karl Marx and Friedrich Engels: *On Colonialism* (Progress Publishers, Moscow) 1968.

MEOB Karl Marx and Friedrich Engels: *On Britain* (Foreign Languages Publishing House, Moscow) 1962.

The Poverty of Philosophy

First published in Brussels in June 1847.

What is, actually, collective wealth, public fortune? It is the wealth of the bourgeoisie—not that of each bourgeois in particular. Well, the economists have done nothing but show how, in the existing relations of production, the wealth of the bourgeoisie has grown and must increase still further. As for the working classes, it still remains a very debatable question as to whether their condition has improved as a result of the increase in so-called public wealth. If economists, in support of their optimism, cite the example of the English workers employed in the cotton industry, they see the condition of the latter only in the rare moments of trade prosperity. These moments of prosperity are, to the periods of crisis and stagnation, in the "true proportion" of 3 to 10. But perhaps also, in speaking of improvement, the economists were thinking of the millions of workers who had to perish in the East Indies so as to procure for the million and a half workers employed in England in the same industry, three years' prosperity out of ten.

Karl Marx: The Poverty of Philosophy
(Martin Lawrence Limited, London 1937), p.85

KARL MARX AND FRIEDRICH ENGELS

Manifesto of the Communist Party

December 1847–January 1848, first published in London in February 1848.

From the serfs of the Middle Ages sprang the chartered burghers of the earliest towns. From these burgesses the first elements of the bourgeoisie were developed.

The discovery of America, the rounding of the Cape, opened up fresh ground for the rising bourgeoisie. The East-Indian and Chinese markets, the colonization of America, trade with the colonies, the increase in the means of exchange and in commodities generally, gave to commerce, to navigation, to industry, an impulse never before known, and thereby, to the revolutionary element in the tottering feudal society, a rapid development. ...

Modern industry has established the world-market, for which the discovery of America paved the way. This market has given an immense development to commerce, to navigation, to communication by land. This development has, in its turn, reacted on the extension of industry; and in proportion as industry, commerce, navigation, railways extended, in the same proportion the bourgeoisie developed, increased its capital, and pushed into the background every class handed down from the Middle Ages ...

The need of a constantly expanding market for its products chases the bourgeoisie over the whole surface of the globe. It must nestle everywhere, settle everywhere, establish connexions everywhere.

The bourgeoisie has through its exploitation of the world-market given a cosmopolitan character to production and consumption

The need of a constantly expanding market for its products chases the bourgeoisie over the whole surface of the globe. It must nestle everywhere, settle everywhere, establish connexions everywhere.

in every country. To the great chagrin of Reactionist, it has drawn from under the feet of industry the national ground on which it stood. All old-established national industries have been destroyed or are daily being destroyed.

They are dislodged by new industries, whose introduction becomes a life and death question for all civilised nations, by industries that no longer work up indigenous raw material, but raw material drawn from the remotest zones; industries whose products are consumed, not only at home, but in every quarter of the globe. In place of the old wants, satisfied by the productions of the country, we find new wants, requiring for their satisfaction the products of distant lands and climes. In place of the old local and national seclusion and self-sufficiency, we have intercourse in every direction, universal inter-dependence of nations. ...

The bourgeoisie, by the rapid improvement of all instruments of production, by the immensely facilitated means of communication, draws all, even the most barbarian, nations into civilisation. The cheap prices of its commodities are the heavy artillery with which it batters down all Chinese walls, with which it forces the barbarians' intensely obstinate hatred of foreigners to capitulate. It compels all nations, on pain of extinction, to adopt the bourgeois mode of production; it compels them to introduce what it calls civilisation into their midst, i.e., to become bourgeois themselves. In one word, it creates a world after its own image.

The bourgeoisie has subjected the country to the rule of the towns. It has created enormous cities, has greatly increased the urban population as compared with the rural, and has thus rescued a considerable part of the population from the idiocy of rural life. Just as it has made the country dependent on the towns, so it has made barbarian and semi-barbarian countries dependent on the civilised ones, nations of peasants on nations of bourgeois, the East on the West.

> **The cheap prices of its commodities are the heavy artillery with which it batters down all Chinese walls ...**

MESW Vol 1, pp. 04-37

Address of the Central Committee to the Communist League

Marx and Engels, March 1850.

Far from desiring to revolutionize all society for the revolutionary proletarians, the democratic petty bourgeois strive for a change in social conditions by means of which existing society will be made as tolerable and comfortable as possible for them. Hence they demand above all diminution of state expenditure by a curtailment of the bureaucracy and shifting the chief taxes on to the big landowners and bourgeois. Further, they demand the abolition of the pressure of big capital on small, through public credit institutions and laws against usury, by which means it will be possible for them and the peasants to obtain advances, on favourable conditions, from the state instead of from the capitalists; they also demand the establishment of bourgeois property relations in the countryside by the complete abolition of feudalism. ...

The domination and speedy increase of capital is further to be counteracted partly by restricting the right of inheritance and partly by transferring as many jobs of work as possible to the state. As far as the workers are concerned, it remains certain above all that they are to remain wageworkers as before; the democratic petty bourgeois only desire better wages and a more secure existence for the workers and hope to achieve this through partial employment by the state and through charity measures; in short, they hope to bribe the workers by more or less concealed alms and to break their revolutionary potency by making their position tolerable for the moment. ... For us the issue cannot be the alteration of private property but only its annihilation, not the smoothing over of class antagonisms but the abolition of classes, not the improvement of existing society but the foundation of a new one.

MESW Vol 1, pp. 101–102

> **For us the issue cannot be the alteration of private property but only its annihilation, not the smoothing over of class antagonisms but the abolition of classes, not the improvement of existing society but the foundation of a new one.**

Revolution in China and in Europe

Written on May 20th, 1853, published in "The New York Daily Tribune" on June 14th, 1853.

Before the British arms the authority of the Manchu dynasty fell to pieces ... and an opening was made for that intercourse which has since proceeded so rapidly under the golden attractions of California and Australia. At the same time the silver coin of the Empire, its lifeblood, began to be drained away to the British East Indies.

Whatever be the social causes and whatever religious, dynastic, or national shape they may assume, that have brought about the chronic rebellions subsisting in China for about ten years past, and now gathered together in one formidable revolution, the occasion of this outbreak has unquestionably been afforded by the English cannon forcing upon China that soporific drug called opium. Before the British arms the authority of the Manchu dynasty fell to pieces; the superstitious faith in the eternity of the Celestial Empire broke down; the barbarous and hermetic isolation from the civilized world was infringed; and an opening was made for that intercourse which has since proceeded so rapidly under the golden attractions of California and Australia.* At the same time the silver coin of the Empire, its lifeblood, began to be drained away to the British East Indies. ...

It is almost needless to observe that, in the same measure in which opium has obtained the sovereignty over the Chinese, the Emperor and his staff of pedantic mandarins have become dispossessed of their own sovereignty. It would seem as though history had first to make this whole people drunk before it could rouse them out of their hereditary stupidity.

Though scarcely existing in former times, the import of English cottons, and to a small extent of English woollens, has rapidly risen since 1833, the epoch when the monopoly of trade

> **The tribute to be paid to England after the unfortunate war of 1840, the great unproductive consumption of opium, the drain of the precious metals by this trade, the destructive influence of foreign competition on native manufactures, the demoralized condition of the public administration ...**

---

* *This refers to emigration of Chinese.*

with China was transferred from the East India Company to private commerce, and on a much greater scale since 1840, the epoch when other nations, and especially our own, also obtained a share in the Chinese trade. This introduction of foreign manufactures has had a similar effect on the native industry to that which it formerly had on Asia Minor, Persia and India. In China the spinners and weavers have suffered greatly under this foreign competition, and the community has become unsettled in proportion.

The tribute to be paid to England after the unfortunate war of 1840, the great unproductive consumption of opium, the drain of the precious metals by this trade, the destructive influence of foreign competition on native manufactures, the demoralized condition of the public administration, produced two things: the old taxation became more burdensome and harassing, and new taxation was added to the old. Thus in a decree of the Emperor, dated Peking, Jan. 5, 1853, we find orders given to the viceroys and governors of the southern provinces of Wuchang and Hanyang to remit and defer the payment of taxes, and especially not in any case to exact more than the regular amount; for otherwise, says the decree, "how

> **All these dissolving agencies acting together on the finances, the morals, the industry, and political structure of China, received their full development under the English cannon in 1840 ...**

will the poor people be able to bear it?"

"And thus, perhaps," continues the Emperor, "will my people, in a period of general hardship and distress, be exempted from the evils of being pursued and worried by the tax-gatherer." Such language as this, and such concessions we remember to have heard from Austria, the China of Germany, in 1848.

All these dissolving agencies acting together on the finances, the morals, the industry, and political structure of China, received their full development under the English cannon in 1840, which broke down the authority of the Emperor, and forced the Celestial Empire into contact with the terrestrial world. Complete isolation was the prime condition of the preservation of old China. That isolation having come to a violent end by the medium of England, dissolution must follow as surely as that of any mummy carefully preserved in a hermetically sealed coffin, whenever it is brought into contact with the open air. Now, England having brought about the revolution of China, the question is how that revolution will in time react on England, and through England on Europe.

MEOC p. 19

The British Rule in India

Written on June 10th, 1853, published in "The New York Daily Tribune" on June 25th, 1853.

All the civil wars, invasions, revolutions, conquests, famines, strangely complex, rapid and destructive as the successive action in Hindostan may appear, did not go deeper than its surface. England has broken down the entire framework of Indian society, without any symptoms of reconstitution yet appearing. This loss of his old world, with no gain of a new one, imparts a particular kind of melancholy to the present misery of the Hindoo, and separates Hindostan, ruled by Britain, from all its ancient traditions, and from the whole of its past history. ...

However changing the political aspect of India's past must

> **It was the British intruder who broke up the Indian hand-loom and destroyed the spinning-wheel. England began with driving the Indian cottons from the European market; it then introduced twist into Hindostan and in the end inundated the very mother country of cotton with cottons.**

appear, its social condition has remained unaltered since its remotest antiquity, until the first decennium of the 19th century. The handloom and the spinning-wheel, producing their regular myriads of spinners and weavers, were the pivots of the structure of that society. ... It was the British intruder who broke up the Indian hand-loom and destroyed the spinning-wheel. England began with driving the Indian cottons from the European market; it then introduced twist into Hindostan and in the end inundated the very mother country of cotton with cottons. From 1818 to 1836 the export of twist from Great Britain to India rose in the proportion of 1 to 5,200. In 1824 the export of British muslin to India hardly amounted to 1,000,000 yards, while in 1837 it surpassed 64,000,000 of yards. But at the same time the population of Dacca decreased from 150,000 inhabitants to 20,000. This decline of Indian towns celebrated for their fabrics was by no means the worst consequence. British steam and science uprooted, over the whole surface of Hindostan, the union between agricultural and manufacturing industry.

These two circumstances—the Hindoo, on the one hand, leaving, like all Oriental peoples, to the central government the care of the great public works, the prime condition of his agriculture and commerce, dispersed, on the other hand over the surface of the country, and agglomerated in small centres by the domestic union of agricultural and manufacturing pursuits—these two circumstances had brought about, since the remotest times, a social system of particular features—the so-called village system, which gave to each of these small unions their independent organisation and distinct life …

These small stereotype forms of social organism have been to the greater part dissolved, and are disappearing, not so much through the brutal interference of the British tax-gatherer and the British soldier, as to the working of English steam and English free trade. Those family-communities were based on domestic industry, in that peculiar combination of hand-weaving, hand-spinning and hand-tilling agriculture which gave them self-supporting power. English interference having placed the spinner in Lancashire and the weaver in Bengal, or sweeping away both Hindoo spinner and weaver, dissolved these small semi-barbarian, semi-civilised communities, by blowing up their economical basis, and thus produced the greatest, and to speak the truth, the only social revolution ever heard of in Asia.

Now, sickening as it must be to human feeling to witness those myriads of industrious patriarchal and inoffensive social organisations disorganised and dissolved into their units, thrown into a sea of woes, and their individual members losing at the same time their ancient form of civilisation, and their hereditary means of subsistence, we must not forget that these idyllic village communities, inoffensive though they may appear, had always been the solid foundation of Oriental despotism, that they restrained the human mind within the smallest possible compass, making it the unresisting tool of superstition, enslaving it beneath traditional rules, depriving it of all grandeur and historical energies. We must not forget the barbarian egotism which, concentrating on some miserable patch of land, had quietly witnessed the ruin of empires, the perpetration of unspeakable cruelties, the massacre of the population of large towns, with no other consideration bestowed upon them than on natural events, itself the helpless prey of any aggressor who deigned to notice it at all. We must not forget that this undignified, stagnatory, and vegetative life, that this passive sort of existence evoked on the other part, in contradistinction, wild, aimless, unbounded forces of destruction and rendered murder itself a religious rite in Hindostan. We must not forget that these little communities were contaminated by distinctions of caste and by slavery, that they subjugated man to external circumstances instead of elevating man to be the sovereign of circumstances, that they transformed a self-developing social state into never changing natural destiny, and thus brought about a brutalising worship of nature, exhibiting its degradation in the fact that man, the sovereign of nature, fell down on his knees in adoration of Kanuman, the monkey, and Sabbala, the cow.

England, it is true, in causing a social revolution in Hindostan, was actuated only by the vilest interests, and was stupid in her manner of enforcing them. But that is not the question. The question is, can mankind fulfill its destiny without a fundamental revolution in the social state of Asia? If not, whatever may have been the crimes of England she was the unconscious tool of history in bringing about that revolution.

MESW Vol 1, pp. 313–317
MEOC pp. 35–41
MEOB pp. 391–398

The Future Results of the British Rule in India

Written on July 22nd, 1853, published in "The New York Daily Tribune" on August 8th, 1853.

England has to fulfill a double mission in India: one destructive, the other regenerating—the annihilation of old Asiatic society, and the laying of the material foundations of Western society in Asia.

Arabs, Turks, Tartars, Moguls, who had successively overrun India, soon became Hindooised, the barbarian conquerors being, by an eternal law of history, conquered themselves by the superior civilisation of their subject. The British were the first conquerors superior, and therefore, inaccessible to Hindoo civilisation. They destroyed it by breaking up the native communities, by uprooting the native industry, and by leveling all that was great and elevated in the native society. The historic pages of their rule in India report hardly anything beyond that destruction. The work of regeneration hardly transpires through a heap of ruins. Nevertheless it has begun. ...

All the English bourgeoisie may be forced to do will neither emancipate nor materially mend the social condition of the mass of the people, depending not only on the development of the productive powers, but of their appropriation by the people. But what they will not fail to do is to lay down the material premises for both. Has the bourgeoisie ever done more? Has it ever effected a progress without dragging individuals and peoples through blood and dirt, through misery and degradation?

The Indians will not reap the fruits of the new elements of society scattered among them by the British bourgeoisie, till in Great Britain itself the now ruling classes shall have been supplanted by the industrial proletariat, or till the Hindoos themselves shall have grown strong enough to throw off the English yoke altogether. ...

The profound hypocrisy and inherent barbarism of bourgeois civilisation lies unveiled before our eyes, turning from its home, where it assumes respectable forms, to the colonies, where it goes naked. They are the defenders of property but did any revolutionary party ever originate agrarian revolutions like those in

> **All the English bourgeoisie may be forced to do will neither emancipate nor materially mend the social condition of the mass of the people, depending not only on the development of the productive powers, but of their appropriation by the people.**

Bengal, in Madras, and in Bombay? Did they not, in India, to borrow an expression of that great robber, Lord Clive himself, resort to atrocious extortion, when simple corruption could not keep pace with their rapacity? While they prated in Europe about the inviolable sanctity of the national debt, did they not confiscate in India the dividends of the rayahs who had invested their private savings in the Company's own funds? While they combatted the French revolution under the pretext of defending "our holy religion," did they not forbid, at the same time, Christianity to be propagated in India, and did they not, in order to make money out of the pilgrims streaming to the temples of Orissa and Bengal, take up the trade in the murder and prostitution perpetrated in the temple of Juggernaut? These are the men of "Property, Order, Family, and Religion."

THE FUTURE RESULTS OF THE BRITISH RULE IN INDIA

The devastating effects of English industry, when contemplated with regard to India, a country as vast as Europe, and containing 150 millions of acres, are palpable and confounding. But we must not forget that they are only the organic results of the whole system of production as it is now constituted. That production rests on the supreme rule of capital. The centralisation of capital is essential to the existence of capital as an independent power. The destructive influence of that centralisation upon the markets of the world does but reveal, in the most gigantic dimensions, the inherent organic laws of political economy now at work in every civilised town. The bourgeois period of history has to create the material basis of the new world—on the one hand the universal intercourse founded upon the mutual dependency of mankind, and the means of that intercourse; on the other hand the development of the productive powers of man and the transformation of material production into a scientific domination of natural agencies. Bourgeois industry and commerce create these material conditions of a new world in the same way as geological revolutions have created the surface of the earth. When a great social revolution shall have mastered the results of the bourgeois epoch, the market of the world and the modern powers of production, and subjected them to the common control of the most advanced peoples, then only will human progress cease to resemble that hideous pagan idol, who would not drink the nectar but from the skulls of the slain.

MSW Vol 1, pp. 320–324
MEOC pp. 81–87
MEOB pp. 399–406

Letter from Engels to Marx

Manchester, May 23rd, 1856.

During our tour in Ireland we came from Dublin to Galway on the west coast, then twenty miles north inland, then to Limerick, down the Shannon to Tarbert, Tralee, Killarney and back to Dublin—a total of about 450 to 500 English miles inside the country itself, so that we have seen about two-thirds of the whole of it. With the exception of Dublin, which bears the same relation to London as Düsseldorf does to Berlin and has quite the character of a small one-time capital, all English-built, too, the look of the entire country, and especially of the towns, is as if one were in France or Northern Italy. Gendarmes, priests, lawyers, bureaucrats, country squires in pleasing profusion and a total absence of any industry at all, so that it would be difficult to understand what all these parasitic growths live on if the distress of the peasants did not supply the other half of the picture.

in France or Northern Italy. Gendarmes, priests, lawyers, bureaucrats, country squires in pleasing profusion and a total absence of any industry at all, so that it would be difficult to understand what all these parasitic growths live on if the distress of the peasants did not supply the other half of the picture. "Strong measures" are visible in every corner of the country, the government meddles with everything, of so-called self-government there is not a trace. Ireland may be regarded as the first English colony and as one which because of its proximity is still governed exactly in the old way, and one can already notice here that the so-called liberty of English citizens is based on the oppression of the colonies. I have never seen so many gendarmes in any country, and the sodden look of the bibulous Prussian gendarme is developed to its highest perfection here among the constabulary, who are armed with carbines, bayonets and handcuffs.

Characteristic of this country are its ruins, the oldest dating from the fifth and sixth centuries, the latest from the nineteenth—with every intervening

> **Ireland may be regarded as the first English colony and as one which because of its proximity is still governed exactly in the old way, and one can already notice here that the so-called liberty of English citizens is based on the oppression of the colonies.**

period. The most ancient are all churches; after 1100, churches and castles; after 1800, houses of peasants. The whole of the west, especially in the neighbourhood of Galway, is covered with ruined peasant houses, most of which have only been deserted since 1846. I never thought that famine could have such tangible reality. Whole villages are devastated, and there among them lie the splendid parks of the lesser landlords, who are almost the only people still living there, mostly lawyers.

Famine, emigration and clearances together have accomplished this. There are not even cattle to be seen in the fields. The land is an utter desert which nobody wants. In County Clare, south of Galway, it is somewhat better. Here there are at least cattle, and the hills towards Limerick are excellently cultivated, mostly by Scottish farmers, the ruins have been cleared away and the country has a bourgeois appearance. In the South-West there are a lot of mountains and bogs but there is also wonderfully luxuriant forest land; beyond that again fine pastures, especially in Tipperary, and towards Dublin there is land which, one can see, is gradually coming into the hands of big farmers.

The country was completely ruined by the English wars of conquest from 1100 to 1850 (for in reality both the wars and the state of siege lasted as long as that). It has been established as a fact that most of the ruins were produced by destruction during the wars. The people itself has got its peculiar character from this, and for all their national Irish fanaticism the fellows feel that they are no longer at home in their own country. Ireland for the Saxon! That is now being realized. The Irishman knows that he cannot compete with the Englishman, who comes equipped with means superior in every respect; emigration will go on until the predominantly, indeed almost exclusively, Celtic character of the population is gone to the dogs. How often have the Irish started out to achieve something, and every time they have been crushed, politically and industrially. By consistent oppression they have been artificially converted into an utterly impoverished nation and now, as everyone knows, fulfill the function of supplying England, America, Australia, etc., with prostitutes, casual labourers, pimps, pickpockets, swindlers, beggars and other rabble. Impoverishment characterizes the aristocracy too. The landowners, who everywhere else have become bourgeoisified, are here reduced to complete poverty. Their country-seats are surrounded by enormous, amazingly beautiful parks, but all around is waste land, and where the money is to come from it is impossible to see. These fellows are droll enough to make your sides burst with laughing. Of mixed blood, mostly tall, strong, handsome chaps, they all wear enormous moustaches under colossal Roman noses, give themselves the false military airs of retired colonels, travel around the country after all sorts of pleasures, and if one makes an inquiry, they haven't a penny, are laden with debts, and live in dread of the Encumbered Estates Court.

Concerning the ways and means by which England rules this country—repression and corruption—long before Bonaparte attempted this, I shall write shortly if you won't come over soon.

MEOC pp. 318–320
MEOB pp. 535–536

English Ferocity in China

Written on March 22nd, 1857, published in "The New York Daily Tribune" on April 10th, 1857.

How silent is the press of England upon the outrageous violations of the treaty daily practised by foreigners living in China under British protection!

We hear nothing of the illicit opium trade, which yearly feeds the British treasury at the expense of human life and morality. We hear nothing of the constant bribery of sub-officials, by means of which the Chinese Government is defrauded of its rightful revenue on incoming and outgoing merchandise. We hear nothing of the wrongs inflicted "even unto death" upon misguided and bonded emigrants sold to worse than slavery on the coast of Peru and into Cuban bondage. We hear nothing of the bullying spirit often exercised against the timid nature of the Chinese, or of the vice introduced by foreigners at the ports open to their trade. We hear nothing of all this and of much more, first, because the majority of people out of China care little about the social and

KARL MARX: ENGLISH FEROCITY IN CHINA

moral condition of that country; and secondly, because it is the part of policy and prudence not to agitate topics where no pecuniary advantage would result. Thus, the English people at home, who look no farther than the grocer's where they buy their tea, are prepared to swallow all the misrepresentations which the Ministry and the Press choose to thrust down the public throat.

Meanwhile, in China, the smothered fires of hatred kindled against the English during their opium war have burst into a flame of animosity, which no tenders of peace and friendship will be very likely to quench.

MEOC p. 115

> ... [T]he English people at home, who look no farther than the grocer's where they buy their tea, are prepared to swallow all the misrepresentations which the Ministry and the Press choose to thrust down the public throat.

Persia and China

Written on May 22nd, 1857.

One thing is certain, that the death-hour of old China is rapidly drawing nigh. Civil war has already divided the South from the North of the Empire, and the Rebel King seems to be as secure from the Imperialists (if not from the intrigues of his own followers) at Nanking, as the Heavenly Emperor from the rebels at Peking. Canton carries on, so far, a sort of independent war with the English, and all foreigners in general; and while British and French fleets and troops flock to Honkong, slowly but steadily the Siberian-line Cossacks advance their *stanitzas** from the Daurian mountains to the banks of the Amur, and the Russian marines close in by fortifications the splendid harbours of Manchuria. The very fanaticism of the southern Chinese in their struggle against foreigners seems to mark a consciousness of the supreme danger in which old China is placed; and before many years pass away, we shall have to witness the death-struggle of the oldest empire in the world, and the opening day of a new era for all Asia.

MEOC p. 125

---

* *Village.*

Letter from Engels to Marx

Manchester, October 7th, 1858.

The business with Jones* is very disgusting. He has held a meeting here and spoken entirely along the lines of the new alliance. After this affair one is really almost driven to believe that the English proletarian movement in its old traditional Chartist form must perish completely before it can develop in a new, viable form. And yet one cannot foresee what this new form will look like. For the rest, it seems to me that Jones's new move, taken in conjunction with the former more or less successful attempts at such an alliance, is really bound up with the fact that the English proletariat is actually becoming more and more bourgeois, so that this most bourgeois of all nations is apparently aiming ultimately at the possession of a bourgeois aristocracy and a bourgeois proletariat alongside the bourgeoisie. For a nation which exploits the whole world this is of course to a certain extent justifiable. The only thing that would help here would be a few thoroughly bad years, but since the gold discoveries these no longer seem so easy to come by.

MESC p. 110
MEOB p. 537

---

* *The Chartist leader Jones tried to form an alliance with the bourgeois Radicals to reform the franchise.*

> ... [T]he English proletariat is actually becoming more and more bourgeois, so that this most bourgeois of all nations is apparently aiming ultimately at the possession of a bourgeois aristocracy and a bourgeois proletariat alongside the bourgeoisie.

Letter from Marx to Engels

London, November 17th, 1862.

England has lately discredited itself more than any other country—the workers by their Christian, slavish nature, the bourgeois and aristocrats by their enthusiasm for slavery in its most direct form. But the two manifestations supplement each other.

MEOB p. 538

The discovery of gold and silver in America, the extirpation, enslavement and entombment in mines of the aboriginal population, the beginning of the conquest and looting of the East Indies, the turning of Africa into a warren for the commercial hunting of black-skins, signalised the rosy dawn of the era of capitalist production.

Capital Vol I, Chapter XXXI

Capital Vol. I published in 1867.

The discovery of gold and silver in America, the extirpation, enslavement and entombment in mines of the aboriginal population, the beginning of the conquest and looting of the East Indies, the turning of Africa into a warren for the commercial hunting of black-skins, signalised the rosy dawn of the era of capitalist production. These idyllic proceedings are the chief momenta of primitive accumulation. On their heels treads the commercial war of the European nations, with the globe for a theatre. It begins with the revolt of the Netherlands from Spain, assumes giant dimensions in England's Anti-Jacobin War, and is still going on in the opium wars against China.

The different momenta of primitive accumulation distribute themselves now, more or less in chronological order, particularly over Spain, Portugal, Holland, France, and England. In England at the end of the 17th century, they arrive at a systematical combination, embracing the colonies, the national debt, the modern mode of taxation, and the protectionist system. These methods depend in part on brute force, e.g., the colonial system. But they all employ the power of the State, the concentrated and organised force of society, to hasten, hot-house fashion, the process of transformation of the feudal mode of production into the capitalist mode, and to shorten the transition. Force is the midwife of every old society pregnant with a new one. It is itself an economic power. ...

The English East India Company, as is well known, obtained besides the political rule in India, the exclusive monopoly of the tea-trade, as well as of the Chinese trade in general, and of the transport of goods to and from Europe. But the coasting trade of India and between the islands, as well as the internal trade of India, were the monopoly of the higher employés of the company. The monopolies of salt, opium, betel and other commodities, were inexhaustible mines of wealth. The employés themselves fixed the price and plundered at will the unhappy Hindus. The Governor-General took part in this private traffic. His favourites received contracts under conditions whereby they, cleverer than alchemists, made gold out of nothing. Great fortunes sprang up like mushrooms in a day; primitive accumulation went on without the advance of a shilling. The trial of Warren Hastings swarms with such cases. Here is an instance. A contract for opium was given to a certain Sullivan at the moment of his departure on an official mission to a part of India far removed from the opium district. Sullivan sold his contract to one Binn for £40,000; Binn sold it the same day for £60,000, and the ultimate purchaser who carried out the contract declared that after all he realised an enormous gain. According to one of the lists laid before Parliament, the Company and its employés from 1757–1766 got £6,000,000 from the Indians as gifts. Between 1769 and 1770, the English manufactured a famine by buying up all the rice and refusing to sell it again, except at fabulous prices. …

> **Between 1769 and 1770, the English manufactured a famine by buying up all the rice and refusing to sell it again, except at fabulous prices.**

KARL MARX: CAPITAL, VOL. I, CHAPTER XXXI

Colonial system, public debts, heavy taxes, protection, commercial wars, etc., these children of the true manufacturing period, increase gigantically during the infancy of Modern Industry. ...

Tantæ molis erat, to establish the "eternal laws of Nature" of the capitalist mode of production, to complete the process of separation between labourers and conditions of labour, to transform, at one pole, the social means of production and subsistence into capital, at the opposite pole, the mass of the population into wage-labourers, into "free labouring poor," that artificial product of modern society. If money, according to Augier, "comes into the world with a congenital blood-stain on one cheek," capital comes dripping from head to foot, from every pore, with blood and dirt.

KMC Vol I, pp. 751–760

> **If money, according to Augier, "comes into the world with a congenital blood-stain on one cheek," capital comes dripping from head to foot, from every pore, with blood and dirt.**

Letter from Marx to Engels

London, November 30th, 1867.

What the English do not yet know is that since 1846 the economic content and therefore also the political aim of English domination in Ireland have entered into an entirely new phase, and that, precisely because of this, Fenianism* is characterized by a socialistic tendency (in a negative sense, directed against the appropriation of the soil) and by being a lower orders movement. What can be more ridiculous than to confuse the barbarities of Elizabeth or Cromwell, who wanted to supplant the Irish by English colonists (in the Roman sense), with the present system, which wants to supplant them by sheep, pigs and oxen! The system of 1801–46, with its rack-rents and middlemen, collapsed in 1846. (During that period evictions were exceptional, occurring mainly in Leinster where the land is especially good for cattle raising.) The repeal of the Corn Laws, partly the result of or at any rate hastened by the Irish famine, deprived Ireland of its monopoly of England's corn supply in normal times. Wool and meat became the slogan, hence conversion of tillage into pasture. Hence from then onwards systematic consolidation of farms. The Encumbered Estates Act, which turned a mass of previously enriched middlemen into landlords, hastened the process. "Clearing of the Estate of Ireland" is now the one purpose of English rule in Ireland. The stupid English Government in London knows nothing of this immense change since 1846. But the Irish

---

* *Fenianism was a petty bourgeois Irish movement organised along clandestine, paramilitary lines. Its main demands were for a Republic and the cancellation of the tenant system.*

> The question now is, what shall we advise the English workers? In my opinion they must make the repeal of the Union ... This is the only legal and therefore only possible form of Irish emancipation which can be admitted in the programme of an English party.

know it. From Meagher's Proclamation (1848) down to the election manifesto of Hennessy (Tory and Urquhartite, 1866), the Irish have expressed their consciousness of it in the clearest and most forcible manner.

The question now is, what shall we advise the English workers? In my opinion they must make the repeal of the Union (in short, the affair of 1783, only democratized and adapted to the conditions of the time) an article of their *pronunziamento*.* This is the only legal and therefore only possible form of Irish emancipation which can be admitted in the programme of an English party. Experience must show later whether a mere personal union can continue to subsist between the two countries. I half think it can if it takes place in time.

What the Irish need is: (1) Self-government and independence from England; (2) An agrarian revolution. With the best intentions

---

* *Declaration of rebellion.*

> **The Union, which overthrew the protective tariffs established by the Irish Parliament, destroyed all industrial life in Ireland.**

in the world the English cannot accomplish this for them, but they can give them the legal means of accomplishing it for themselves; (3) Protective tariffs against England.

Between 1783 and 1801 every branch of Irish industry flourished. The Union, which overthrew the protective tariffs established by the Irish Parliament, destroyed all industrial life in Ireland. The bit of linen industry is no compensation whatever. The Union of 1801 had just the same effect on Irish industry as the measures for the suppression of the Irish woollen industry, etc., taken by the English Parliament under Anne, George II, and others. Once the Irish are independent, necessity will turn them into protectionists, as it did Canada, Australia, etc.

MESC p. 195
MEOC p. 326
MEOB p. 542

Letter from Marx to Kugelmann

London, April 6th, 1868.

The Irish question predominates here just now. It has been exploited by Gladstone and company, of course, only in order to get into office again, and, above all, to have an electoral cry at the next elections, which will be based on household suffrage. For the moment this turn of affairs is bad for the workers' party; the intriguers among the workers, such as Odger and Potter, who want to get into the next Parliament, have now a new excuse for attaching themselves to the bourgeois Liberals.

However, this is only a penalty which England—and consequently also the English working class—is paying for the great crime it has been committing for many centuries against Ireland.

> ... [T]he intriguers among the workers ... who want to get into the next Parliament, have now a new excuse for attaching themselves to the bourgeois Liberals. However, this is only a penalty which England—and consequently also the English working class—is paying for the great crime it has been committing for many centuries against Ireland.

And in the long run it will benefit the English working class itself. You see, the English Established Church in Ireland—or what they call here the Irish Church—is the religious bulwark of English landlordism in Ireland, and at the same time the outpost of the Established Church in England itself. (I am speaking here of the Established Church as a landowner.) The overthrow of the Established Church in Ireland will mean its downfall in England and the two will be followed by the doom of landlordism—first in Ireland and then in England. I have, however, been convinced from the first that the social revolution must begin seriously from the bottom, that is, from landownership.

Apart from that, the whole thing will have the very useful result that, once the Irish Church is dead, the Protestant Irish tenants in the province of Ulster will make common cause with the Catholic tenants in the three other provinces of Ireland, whereas up to the present landlordism has been able to exploit this religious antagonism.

MESC p. 203
MEOC p. 328
MEOB p. 544

Letter from Engels to Marx

Manchester, November 18th, 1868.

What do you say to the elections in the factory districts? Once again the proletariat has discredited itself terribly. Manchester and Salford return three Tories* to two Liberals, including moreover the milk-and-water Bazley, Bolton, Preston, Blackburn, etc., practically nothing but Tories. In Ashton it looks as if M. Gibson went to the wall. Ernest Jones nowhere, despite the cheering. Everywhere the proletariat is the tag, rag and bobtail of the official parties, and if any party has gained strength from the new voters, it is the Tories. The small towns, the half-rotten boroughs, are the salvation of bourgeois liberalism and the roles will be reversed: the Tories will now be in favour of more members for the big towns and the Liberals for unequal representation.

Here (Manchester) the electors have increased from 24,000 to quite 48,000, while the Tories have increased their voters from 6,000 to 14,000–15,000. The Liberals allowed much to slip by them and Mr. Henry did a lot of damage, but it cannot be denied that the increase of working-class voters has brought the Tories more than their simple percentage increase; it has improved their relative position. On the whole this is to the good. It looks at present as if Gladstone will get a narrow majority and so be compelled to keep the ball rolling and reform the Reform Act; with a big majority he would have left it all to Providence as usual.

---

* *English bourgeois political party stemming from 1679 when Charles II's followers created a party under the name of Tory; in connection with the Reform Bill of 1832 the name was changed to the Conservative Party.*

LETTER FROM ENGELS TO MARX, NOVEMBER 18, 1868

But it remains a disastrous certificate of poverty for the English proletariat all the same. The parson has shown unexpected power and so has the cringing to respectability. Not a single working-class candidate had a ghost of a chance, but my Lord Tumnoddy or any parvenu snob could have the workers' votes with pleasure.

The clamour of the liberal bourgeois would amuse me greatly were it not for this collateral circumstance.

MEOB p. 545

Letter from Engels to Marx

Manchester, October 24th, 1869.

Irish history shows one how disastrous it is for a nation when it has subjected another nation. All the abominations of the English have their origin in the Irish Pale.*

I have still to work through the Cromwellian period, but this much seems certain to me, that things would have taken another turn in England but for the necessity for military rule in Ireland and the creation of a new aristocracy there.

MESC p. 222
MEOC p. 329
MEOB p. 546

> **Irish history shows one how disastrous it is for a nation when it has subjected another nation. All the abominations of the English have their origin in the Irish Pale.**

---

* *The eastern part of Ireland which was conquered by the British during the 12th century, and which formed a bridgehead for the conquest of the whole of Ireland during the 15th century.*

Letter from Marx to Kugelmann

London, November 29th, 1869.

Nevertheless, both my utterance on this Irish amnesty question and my further proposal to the General Council to discuss the attitude of the English working class to Ireland and to pass resolutions on it have of course other objects besides that of speaking out loudly and decidedly for the oppressed Irish against their oppressors.

I have become more and more convinced—and the only question is to drive this conviction home to the English working class—that it can never do anything decisive here in England until it separates its policy with regard to Ireland most definitely from the policy of the ruling classes, until it not only makes common cause with the Irish but actually takes the initiative in dissolving the Union established in 1801* and replacing it by a free federal relationship. And this must be done, not as a matter of sympathy with Ireland but as a demand made in the interests of the English proletariat. If not, the English people will remain tied to the leading-strings of the ruling classes, because it will have to join with them in a common front against Ireland. Every one of its movements in England itself is crippled by the strife with the Irish, who form a very important section of the working class in England. The prime condition of emancipation here—the overthrow of the English landed oligarchy—remains impossible because its position here cannot

---

* *In 1800 the British Parliament passed the law of the Union, whereby Ireland was forcefully incorporated into England and the Irish Parliament dissolved. The Union became effective as of January 1, 1801.*

... [T]he English people will remain tied to the leading-strings of the ruling classes, because it will have to join with them in a common front against Ireland. Every one of its movements in England itself is crippled by the strife with the Irish ... The prime condition of emancipation here—the overthrow of the English landed oligarchy—remains impossible because its position here cannot be stormed so long as it maintains its strongly entrenched outposts in Ireland.

be stormed so long as it maintains its strongly entrenched outposts in Ireland. But there, once affairs are in the hands of the Irish people itself, once it is made its own legislator and ruler, once it becomes autonomous, the abolition of the landed aristocracy (to a large extent the same persons as the English landlords) will be infinitely easier than here, because in Ireland it is not merely a simple economic question but at the same time a national question, since the landlords there are not, like those in England, the traditional dignitaries and representatives of the nation, but its mortally hated oppressors. And not only does England's internal social development remain

... [I]n Ireland it is not merely a simple economic question but at the same time a national question, since the landlords there are not, like those in England, the traditional dignitaries and representatives of the nation, but its mortally hated oppressors.

crippled by her present relations with Ireland; her foreign policy, and particularly her policy with regard to Russia and the United States of America, suffers the same fate.

But since the English working class undoubtedly throws the decisive weight into the scale of social emancipation generally, the lever has to be applied here. As a matter of fact, the English republic under Cromwell met shipwreck in—Ireland. *Non bis in idem!** But the Irish have played a capital joke on the English government by electing the "convict felon" O'Donovan Rossa to Parliament. The government papers are already threatening a renewed suspension of the Habeas Corpus Act, a renewed system of terror. In fact, England never has and never can—so long as the present relations last—rule Ireland otherwise than by the most abominable reign of terror and the most reprehensible corruption.

MESC p. 229

---

* *Not twice the same thing!*

Letter from Marx to Engels
London, December 10th, 1869.

The way I shall put forward the matter next Tuesday is this: that quite apart from all phrases about "international" and "humane" justice for Ireland—which are taken for granted in the International Council—it is in the direct and absolute interest of the English working class to get rid of their present connection with Ireland. And this is my fullest conviction, and for reasons which in part I cannot tell the English workers themselves. For a long time I believed that it would be possible to overthrow the Irish regime by English working-class ascendancy. I always expressed this point of view in the *New York Tribune*. Deeper study has now convinced me of the opposite. The English working class will never accomplish anything until it has got rid of Ireland. The lever must be applied in Ireland. That is why the Irish question is so important for the social movement in general.

MESC p. 231
MEOC p. 332

Letter from Marx to Meyer and Vogt

London, April 9th, 1870.

Among the material sent you will also find some of the resolutions of the General Council of November 30 on the Irish amnesty, resolutions that you know about and that were written by me; likewise an Irish pamphlet on the treatment of the Fenian* convicts.

I had intended to introduce additional resolutions on the necessary transformation of the present Union (i.e., enslavement of Ireland) into a free and equal federation with Great Britain. For the time being, further progress in this matter, as far as public

> After occupying myself with the Irish question for many years I have come to the conclusion that the decisive blow against the English ruling classes (and it will be decisive for the workers' movement all over the world) cannot be delivered in England but only in Ireland.

---

* *On September 18 an attack was made at a prison in Manchester in order to free two Fenian leaders, Kelley and Deasy. They escaped, but others were captured and later sentenced to death and executed for having killed a policeman.*

resolutions go, has been suspended because of my enforced absence from the General Council. No other member of it has sufficient knowledge of Irish affairs and adequate prestige with its English members to be able to replace me here.

Meanwhile time has not been spent idly and I ask you to pay particular attention to the following:

After occupying myself with the Irish question for many years I have come to the conclusion that the decisive blow against the English ruling classes (and it will be decisive for the workers' movement all over the world) cannot be delivered in England but only in Ireland.

On January 1, 1870, the General Council issued a confidential circular drawn up by me in French (for the reaction upon England only the French, not the German, papers are important) on the relation of the Irish national struggle to the emancipation of the working class, and therefore on the attitude

The exploitation of that country is not only one of the main sources of this aristocracy's material welfare; it is its greatest moral strength. It, in fact, represents the domination of England over Ireland. Ireland is therefore the great means by which the English aristocracy maintains its domination in England itself.

which the International Association should take in regard to the Irish question.

I shall give you here only quite briefly the decisive points.

Ireland is the bulwark of the English landed aristocracy. The exploitation of that country is not only one of the main sources of this aristocracy's material welfare; it is its greatest moral strength. It, in fact, represents the domination of England over Ireland. Ireland is therefore the great means by which the English aristocracy maintains its domination in England itself.

The destruction of the English landed aristocracy in Ireland is an infinitely easier operation than in England itself ... because it is a question of existence, of life and death, for the immense majority of the Irish people, and because it is at the same time inseparable from the national question.

If, on the other hand, the English army and police were to withdraw from Ireland tomorrow, you would at once have an agrarian revolution there. But the overthrow of the English aristocracy in Ireland involves as a necessary consequence its overthrow in England. And this would fulfil the preliminary condition for the proletarian revolution in England. The destruction of the English landed aristocracy in Ireland is an infinitely easier operation than in England itself, because in Ireland the land question has hitherto been the exclusive form of the social question, because it is a question of existence, of life and death, for the immense majority of the Irish people, and because it is at the same time inseparable from the national question. This quite apart from the Irish being more passionate and revolutionary in character than the English.

As for the English bourgeoisie, it has in the first place a common interest with the English aristocracy in turning Ireland into mere pasture land which provides the English market with meat and wool at the cheapest possible prices. It is equally interested in reducing, by eviction and forcible emigration, the Irish population to such a small number that English capital (capital invested in land leased for farming) can function there with "security." It has the same interest in clearing the estate of Ireland as it had in the clearing of the agricultural districts of England and Scotland. The £6,000–10,000 absentee-landlord and other Irish revenues which at present flow annually to London have also to be taken into account.

But the English bourgeoisie has, besides, much more important interests in Ireland's present-day economy.

Owing to the constantly increasing concentration of tenant-farming, Ireland steadily supplies its own surplus to the English labour market, and thus forces down wages and lowers the moral and material condition of the English working class.

And most important of all! Every industrial and commercial centre in England now possesses a working class divided into two hostile camps, English proletarians and Irish proletarians. The ordinary English worker hates the Irish worker as a competitor who lowers his standard of life. In relation to the Irish worker he feels himself a member of the ruling nation and so turns himself into a tool of the aristocrats and capitalists of his country against Ireland, thus strengthening their domination over himself. He cherishes religious, social, and national prejudices against the Irish worker. His attitude towards him is much the same as that of the "poor whites" to the "niggers" in the former slave states of the U.S.A. The Irishman pays him back with interest in his own money. He sees in the English worker at once the accomplice and the stupid tool of the English rule in Ireland.

This antagonism is artificially kept alive and intensified by the press, the pulpit, the comic papers, in short, by all the means at the disposal of the ruling classes. This antagonism is the secret of the impotence of the English working class, despite its organisation. It is the secret by which the capitalist class maintains its power. And that class is fully aware of it.

Every industrial and commercial centre in England now possesses a working class divided into two hostile camps, English proletarians and Irish proletarians. The ordinary English worker hates the Irish worker as a competitor who lowers his standard of life.

But the evil does not stop here. It continues across the ocean. The antagonism between English and Irish is the hidden basis of the conflict between the United States and England. It makes any honest and serious co-operation between the working classes of the two countries impossible. It enables the governments of both countries, whenever they think fit, to break the edge off the social conflict by their mutual bullying, and, in case of need, by war with one another.

England, being the metropolis of capital, the power which has hitherto ruled the world market, is for the present the most important country for the workers' revolution, and moreover the only country in which the material conditions for this revolution have developed up to a certain degree of maturity. Therefore to hasten the social revolution in England is the most important object of

> **In relation to the Irish worker [the English worker] feels himself a member of the ruling nation and so turns himself into a tool of the aristocrats and capitalists of his country against Ireland ... He cherishes religious, social, and national prejudices against the Irish worker. His attitude towards him is much the same as that of the "poor whites" to the "niggers" in the former slave states of the U.S.A.**

the International Workingmen's Association. The sole means of hastening it is to make Ireland independent.

Hence it is the task of the International everywhere to put the conflict between England and Ireland in the foreground, and everywhere to side openly with Ireland. And it is the special task of the Central Council in London to awaken a consciousness in the English workers that for them the national emancipation of Ireland is no question of abstract justice or humanitarian sentiment but the first condition of their own social emancipation.

MESC p. 235
MEOC p. 335
MEOB p. 550

> **Hence it is the task of the International everywhere to put the conflict between England and Ireland in the foreground, and everywhere to side openly with Ireland ... [and] to awaken a consciousness in the English workers that for them the national emancipation of Ireland is no question of abstract justice or humanitarian sentiment ...**

The English Elections

Written on February 22nd, 1874, published in "Der Volksstaat."

As regards the workers it must be stated, to begin with, that no separate political working-class party has existed in England since the downfall of the Chartist Party in the fifties. This is understandable in a country in which the working-class has shared more than anywhere else in the advantages of the immense expansion of its large-scale industry. Nor could it have been otherwise in an England that ruled the world market; and certainly not in a country where the ruling classes have set themselves the task of carrying out, parallel with other concessions, one point of the Chartists' programme, the People's Charter, after another. Of the six points of the Charter two have already become law: the secret ballot and the abolition of property qualifications for the suffrage. The third, universal suffrage, has been introduced, at least approximately; the last three points are still entirely unfulfilled: annual parliaments, payment of members, and most important, equal electoral areas.

Whenever the workers lately took part in general politics in particular organisations they did so almost exclusively as the extreme left wing of the "great Liberal Party" and in this role they were duped at each election according to all the rules of the game by the great Liberal Party. Then all of a sudden came the Reform Bill which at one blow changed the political status of the workers. In all the big cities they now form the majority of the voters and in England the Government as well as the candidates for Parliament are accustomed to court the electorate. The chairmen and secretaries of Trade Unions and political workingmen's societies, as well as other well-known labour spokesmen who might be expected to be influential in their class, had overnight become important people.

They were visited by Members of Parliament, by lords and other well-born rabble, and sympathetic enquiry was suddenly made into the wishes and needs of the working-class. Questions were discussed with these "labour leaders" which formerly evoked a supercilious smile or the mere posture of which used to be condemned; and one contributed to collections for working-class purposes. It thereupon quite naturally occurred to the "labour leaders" that they should get themselves elected to Parliament, to which their high-class friends gladly agreed in general, but of course only for the purpose of frustrating as far as possible the election of workers in each particular case. Thus the matter got no further.

Nobody holds it against the "labour leaders" that they would have liked to get into Parliament. The shortest way would have been to proceed at once to form anew a strong workers' party with a definite programme, and the best political programme they could wish for was the People's Charter. But the Chartists' name was in bad odour with the bourgeoisie precisely because theirs had been an outspokenly proletarian party, and so, rather than continue the glorious tradition of the Chartists, the "labour leaders" preferred to deal with their aristocratic friends and be "respectable," which in England means acting like a bourgeois. Whereas under the old franchise the workers had to a certain extent been compelled to figure as the tail of the radical bourgeoisie, it was inexcusable to make them go on playing that

> **Then all of a sudden came the Reform Bill which at one blow changed the political status of the workers ...**
>
> **The chairmen and secretaries of Trade Unions and political workingmen's societies, as well as other well-known labour spokesmen who might be expected to be influential in their class, had overnight become important people.**

part after the Reform Bill had opened the door of Parliament to at least sixty working-class candidates.

This was the turning point. In order to get into Parliament the "labour leaders" had recourse, in the first place, to the votes and money of the bourgeoisie and only in the second place to the votes of the workers themselves. But by doing so they ceased to be workers' candidates and turned themselves into bourgeois candidates. They did not appeal to a working-class party that still had to be formed but to the bourgeois "great Liberal Party." …

MEOB p. 503

> … [R]ather than continue the glorious tradition of the Chartists, the "labour leaders" preferred to deal with their aristocratic friends and be "respectable," which in England means acting like a bourgeois.

Letter from Marx to Liebknecht

London, February 11th, 1878.

The English working-class had been gradually becoming more and more deeply demoralised by the period of corruption since 1848 and had at last got to the point when it was nothing more than the tail of the Great Liberal Party, i.e., of its oppressors, the capitalists. Its direction had passed completely into the hands of the venal trade-union leaders and professional agitators. These fellows shouted and howled behind the Gladstones, Brights, Mundellas, Morleys and the whole gang of factory owners, etc., in *majorem gloriam** of the tsar as the emancipator of nations, while they never raised a finger for their own brothers in South Wales, condemned by the mine-owners to die of starvation. Wretches! To crown the whole affair worthily, in the last divisions in the House of Commons (on February 7 and 8, when the majority of the high dignitaries of the "Great Liberal Party"—the Forsters, Lowes, Harcourts, Goschens, Hartingtons and even the great John Bright himself—left their army in the lurch and bolted away from the division in order not to compromise themselves too much by voting) the only workers' representatives there and moreover, *horribile dictu*,** direct representatives of the miners, and themselves originally miners—Burt and the miserable MacDonald—voted with the rump of the "great Liberal Party" ...

MESC p. 314
MEOB p. 554

---

* *To the greater glory.*   ** *Horrible to relate.*

Letter from Engels to Bernstein

London, June 17th, 1879.

For a number of years past (and at the present time) the English working-class movement has been hopelessly describing a narrow circle of strikes for higher wages and shorter hours, not, however, as an expedient or means of propaganda and organisation but as the ultimate aim. The Trade Unions even bar all political action on principle and in their charters, and thereby also ban participation in any general activity of the working-class as a class. The workers are divided politically into Conservatives and Liberal Radicals, into supporters of the Disraeli (Beaconsfield) ministry and supporters of the Gladstone ministry. One can speak here of a labour movement (proper) only in so far as strikes take place here which, whether they are won or not, do not get the movement one step further. To inflate such strikes—which often enough have been brought about purposely during the last few years of bad business by the capitalists to have a pretext for closing down their factories and mills, strikes in which the working-class movement does not make the slightest headway—into struggles of world importance, as is done, for instance, in the London *Freiheit*, can, in my opinion, only do harm. No attempt should be made to conceal the fact that at present no real labour movement in the continental sense exists here, and I therefore believe you will not lose much if for the time being you do not receive any reports on the doings of the Trade Unions here.

MESC p. 320
MEOB p. 555

LETTER FROM ENGELS TO BERNSTEIN, JUNE 17, 1879

> For a number of years ...
> the English working-class
> movement has been hopelessly
> describing a narrow circle of
> strikes for higher wages and
> shorter hours, not, however,
> as an expedient or means of
> propaganda and organisation
> but as the ultimate aim.

Letter from Marx to Danielson

London, February 19th, 1881.

In India serious complications, if not a general outbreak, is in store for the British government. What the English take from them annually in the form of rent, dividends for railways useless to the Hindus; pensions for military and civil servicemen, for Afghanistan and other wars, etc., etc.—what they take from them without any equivalent and quite apart from what they appropriate to themselves annually within India—speaking only of the value of the commodities the Indians have gratuitously and annually to send over to England—it amounts to more than the total sum of income of the sixty millions of agricultural and industrial labourers of India! This is a bleeding process, with a vengeance! The famine years are pressing each other and in dimensions till now not yet suspected in Europe! There is an actual conspiracy going on wherein Hindus and Mussulmans co-operate; the British government is aware that something is "brewing," but this shallow people (I mean the governmental men), stultified by their own parliamentary ways of talking and thinking, do not even desire to see clear, to realise the whole extent of the imminent danger! To delude others and by deluding them to delude yourself—this is: parliamentary wisdom in a nutshell! *Tant mieux!**

MESC p. 336
MEOC p. 339
MEOB p. 557

---

* *So much the better!*

Letter from Engels to Kautsky

London, September 12th, 1882.

You ask me what the English workers think about colonial policy. Well, exactly the same as they think about politics in general: the same as the bourgeois think. There is no workers' party here, you see, there are only Conservatives and Liberal-Radicals, and the workers gaily share the feast of England's monopoly of the world market and the colonies. In my opinion the colonies proper, i.e., the countries occupied by a European population, Canada, the Cape, Australia, will all become independent; on the other hand, the countries inhabited by a native population, which are simply subjugated, India, Algeria, the Dutch, Portuguese and Spanish possessions, must be taken over for the time being by the proletariat and led as rapidly as possible towards independence. How this process will develop is difficult to say. India will perhaps, indeed very probably, make a revolution, and as a proletariat in process of self-emancipation cannot conduct any colonial wars, it would have to be allowed to run its course; it would not pass off without all sorts of destruction, of course, but that sort of thing is inseparable from all revolutions. The same might also take place elsewhere, e.g., in Algeria and Egypt, and would certainly be the best thing for us. We shall have enough to do at home. Once Europe is re-organised, and North America, that will furnish such colossal power and such an example that the semi-civilised countries will follow in their wake of their own accord; economic needs, if anything, will see to that. But as to what social and political phases these countries will then have to pass through before they likewise arrive at socialist organisation, I think we to-day can advance only rather idle hypotheses. One thing alone is certain: the victorious proletariat can force no blessings of any kind upon any foreign nation without undermining its own victory by so doing. Which of course by no means excludes defensive wars of various kinds.

MESC p. 351

Letter from Engels to Bebel

Eastbourne, August 30th, 1883.

The Manifesto of the Democratic Federation in London has been issued by about twenty to thirty little societies, which under different names (always the same people) have for the last twenty years at least been repeatedly trying, and always with the same lack of success, to make themselves important. The only thing important is that now at last they are obliged openly to proclaim our theory as their own, whereas during the period of the International it seemed to them to be foisted on them from outside, and that recently a lot of young people stemming from the bourgeoisie have appeared on the scene who; to the disgrace of the English workers it must be said, understand things better and take them up more enthusiastically than the workers themselves. For even in the Democratic Federation the workers for the most part accept the new programme only unwillingly and as a matter of form. The leader of the

> **Do not on any account whatever let yourself be bamboozled into thinking there is a real proletarian movement going on here ... a really general workers' movement will come into existence here only when the workers feel that England's world monopoly is broken.**

Democratic Federation, Hyndman, is an arch-conservative and an arrantly chauvinistic but not stupid careerist, who behaved pretty shabbily to Marx (to whom he had been introduced by Rudolf Meyer) and for this reason was dropped by us personally.

Do not on any account whatever let yourself be bamboozled into thinking there is a real proletarian movement going on here. I know Liebknecht is trying to delude himself and all the world about this,

> **Participation in the domination of the world market was and is the economic basis of the political nullity of the English workers. The tail of the bourgeoisie in the economic exploitation of this monopoly but nevertheless sharing in its advantages, they are, of course, politically the tail-of the "Great Liberal Party" ...**

but it is not the case. The elements at present active may become important now that they have accepted our theoretical programme and so acquired a basis, but only if a spontaneous movement breaks out here among the workers and they succeed in getting control of it. Till then they will remain individual minds, with a hotch-potch of confused sects; remnants of the great movement of the 'forties, standing behind them, and nothing more. And—apart from the unexpected—a really general workers' movement will come into existence here only when the workers feel that England's world monopoly is broken.

Participation in the domination of the world market was and is the economic basis of the political nullity of the English workers. The tail of the bourgeoisie in the economic exploitation of this monopoly but nevertheless sharing in its advantages, they are, of course, politically the tail of the "Great Liberal Party," which for its part pays them small attentions, recognises Trade Unions and strikes as legitimate factors, has abandoned the fight for an unlimited working-day and has given the mass of better-off workers the vote. But once America and the joint competition of the other industrial countries make a big enough breach in this monopoly (and in iron this is coming rapidly, in cotton unfortunately not as yet) you will see a lot of things happen here.

MESC p. 364
MEOB p. 561

Friedrich Engels: England in 1845 and in 1885

Published on March 1st, 1885, in "Commonweal," quoted in "Preface to 'The Condition of The Working-Class in England'" on July 21st, 1892.

Forty years ago England stood face to face with a crisis, solvable to all appearances by force only. The immense and rapid development of manufactures had outstripped the extension of foreign markets and the increase of demand. Every ten years the march of industry was violently interrupted by a general commercial crash, followed, after a long period of chronic depression, by a few short years of prosperity, and always ending in feverish over-production and consequent renewed collapse. The capitalist class clamoured for Free Trade in corn, and threatened to enforce it by sending the starving population of the towns back to the country districts whence they came, to invade them, as John Bright said, not as paupers begging for bread, but as an army quartered upon the enemy. The working masses of the towns demanded their

> **England was to become the "workshop of the world"; all other countries were to become for England what Ireland already was—markets for her manufactured goods, supplying her in return with raw materials and food.**

share of political power—the People's Charter; they were supported by the majority of the small trading class, and the only difference between the two was whether the Charter should be carried by physical or by moral force. Then came the commercial crash of 1847 and the Irish famine, and with both the prospect of revolution.

The French Revolution of 1848 saved the English middle-class. The Socialistic pronunciamentos of the victorious French workmen frightened the small middle-class of England and disorganised the narrower, but more matter-of-fact movement of the English working-class. At the very moment when Chartism was bound to assert itself in its full strength, it collapsed internally before even it collapsed externally, on the 10th of April, 1848. The action of the working-class was thrust into the background. The capitalist class triumphed along the whole line.

The Reform Bill of 1831 had been the victory of the whole capitalist class over the landed aristocracy. The repeal of the Corn Laws was the victory of the manufacturing capitalist not only over the landed aristocracy, but over those sections of capitalists, too, whose interests were more or less bound up with the landed interest—bankers, stock-jobbers,

England, the great manufacturing centre of an agricultural world, with an ever-increasing number of corn and cotton-growing Irelands revolving around her, the industrial sun. What a glorous prospect!

fund-holders, etc. Free Trade meant the readjustment of the whole home and foreign, commercial and financial policy of England in accordance with the interests of the manufacturing capitalists—the class which now represented the nation. And they set about this task with a will. Every obstacle to industrial production was mercilessly removed. The tariff and the whole system of taxation were revolutionised. Everything was made subordinate to one end, but that end of the utmost importance to the manufacturing capitalist: the cheapening of all raw produce, and especially of the means of living of the working-class; the reduction of the cost of raw material, and the keeping down—if not as yet the bringing down—of wages. England was to become the "workshop of the world"; all other countries were to become for England what Ireland already was—markets for her manufactured goods, supplying her in return with raw materials and food. England, the great manufacturing centre of an agricultural world, with an ever-increasing number of corn and cotton-growing Irelands revolving around her, the industrial sun. What a glorious prospect!

The manufacturing capitalists set about the realisation of this their great object with that strong common sense and that contempt for traditional principles which has ever distinguished them from their more narrow-minded compeers on the Continent. Chartism was dying out. The revival of commercial prosperity, natural after the revulsion of 1847 had spent itself, was put down altogether to the credit of Free Trade. Both these circumstances had turned the English working-class, politically, into the tail of the "great Liberal Party," the party led by the manufacturers. This advantage, once gained, had to be perpetuated. And the manufacturing capitalists from the Chartist opposition, not to Free Trade, but to the transformation of Free Trade into the one vital national question, had learnt, and were learning more and more, that the middle-class can never obtain full social and political power over the nation except by the help of the working-class. Thus a gradual change came over the relations between both classes. The Factory Acts, once the bugbear of all manufacturers, were not only willingly submitted to, but their expansion into acts regulating almost all trades was tolerated. Trades' Unions, hitherto considered inventions of the devil himself, were now petted and patronised as perfectly legitimate institutions, and as useful means of spreading sound economical

Trades' Unions, hitherto considered inventions of the devil himself, were now petted and patronised as perfectly legitimate institutions, and as useful means of spreading sound economical doctrines amongst the workers. Even strikes, than which nothing had been more nefarious up to 1848, were now gradually found out to be occasionally very useful, especially when provoked by the masters themselves, at their own time.

doctrines amongst the workers. Even strikes, than which nothing had been more nefarious up to 1848, were now gradually found out to be occasionally very useful, especially when provoked by the masters themselves, at their own time. Of the legal enactments, placing the workman at a lower level or at a disadvantage with regard to the master, at least the most revolting were repealed. And, practically, that horrid "People's Charter" actually became the political programme of the very manufacturers who had opposed it to the last. "The Abolition of the Property Qualification" and "Vote by Ballot" are now the law of the land. The Reform Acts of 1867 and 1884 make a near approach to "universal suffrage," at least such as it now exists in Germany; the Redistribution Bill now before Parliament creates "equal electoral districts"—on the whole not more unequal than those of Germany; "payment of members," and shorter, if not actually "annual Parliaments," are visibly looming in the distance—and yet there are people who say that Chartism is dead.

The Revolution of 1848, not less than many of its predecessors, has had strange bedfellows and successors. The very people who put it down have become, as Karl Marx used to say, its testamentary executors. Louis Napoleon had to create an independent and united Italy, Bismarck had to revolutionise Germany and to restore Hungarian independence, and the English manufacturers had to enact the People's Charter.

For England, the effects of this domination of the manufacturing capitalists were at first startling. Trade revived and extended to a degree unheard of even in this cradle of modern industry; the previous astounding creations of steam and machinery dwindled into nothing compared with the immense mass of productions of the twenty years from 1850 to 1870, with the overwhelming figures of exports and imports, of wealth accumulated in the hands of capitalists and of human working power concentrated in the large towns. The progress was indeed interrupted, as before, by a crisis every ten years, in 1857 as well as in 1866; but these revulsions were now considered as natural, inevitable events, which must be fatalistically submitted to, and which always set themselves right in the end.

And the condition of the working-class during this period? There was temporary improvement even for the great mass. But this improvement always was reduced to the old level by the influx of the great body of the unemployed reserve, by the constant superseding of hands by new machinery, by the immigration of the agricultural population, now, too, more and more superseded by machines.

A permanent improvement can be recognised for two "protected" sections only of the working-class. Firstly, the factory hands. The fixing by Act of Parliament of their working-day within relatively rational limits has restored their physical constitution and endowed them with a moral superiority, enhanced by their local concentration. They are undoubtedly better off than before 1848. The best proof is that, out of ten strikes they make, nine are provoked by the manufacturers in their own interests, as the only means of securing a reduced production. You can never get the masters to agree to work "short time," let manufactured goods be ever so unsaleable; but get the workpeople to strike, and the masters shut their factories to a man.

Secondly, the great Trades Unions. They are the organisations of those trades in which the labour of grown-up men predominates, or is alone applicable. Here the competition, neither of women and children nor of machinery has so far weakened their organised strength. The engineers, the carpenters and joiners, the bricklayers, are each of them a power; to that extent that, as in the case of the bricklayers and bricklayers' labourers, they can even successfully resist the introduction of machinery. That their condition has remarkably improved since 1848 there can be no doubt, and the best proof of this is in the fact that for more than fifteen years not only have their employers been with them, but they with their employers, upon exceedingly good terms. They form an aristocracy among the working-class; they have succeeded in enforcing for themselves a relatively comfortable position, and they accept it as final. They are the model working-men of Messrs. Leone Levi & Giffen, and they are very nice people indeed nowadays to deal with, for any sensible capitalist in particular and for the whole capitalist class in general.

But as to the great mass of working-people, the state of misery and insecurity in which they live now is as low as ever, if not lower. The East End of London is an everspreading pool of stagnant misery and desolation, of starvation when out of work, and degradation, physical and moral, when in work. And so in all other large towns—abstraction made of the privileged minority of the workers; and so in the smaller towns and in the agricultural districts. The law which reduces the value of labour-power to the value of the necessary means of subsistence, and the other law which reduces its average price, as a rule, to the minimum of those means of subsistence, these laws act upon them with the irresistible force of an automatic engine which crushes them between its wheels.

This, then, was the position created by the Free Trade policy of 1847, and by twenty years of the rule of the manufacturing capitalists. But then a change came. The crash of 1866 was, indeed, followed by a slight and short revival about 1873; but that did not last. We did not, indeed, pass through the full crisis at the time it was due, in 1877 or 1878; but we have had, ever since 1876, a chronic state of stagnation in all dominant branches of industry. Neither will the full crash come; nor will the period of longed-for prosperity to which we used to be entitled before and after it. A dull depression, a chronic glut of all markets for all trades, that is what we have been living in for nearly ten years. How is this?

The Free Trade theory was based upon one assumption: that England was to be the one great manufacturing centre of an agricultural world. And the actual fact is that this assumption has turned out to be a pure delusion. The conditions of modern industry, steam-power and machinery, can be established wherever there is fuel, especially coals. And other countries besides England— France, Belgium, Germany, America, even Russia—have coals. And the people over there did not see the advantage of being turned into Irish pauper farmers merely for the greater wealth and glory of English capitalists. They set resolutely about manufacturing, not only for themselves, but for the rest of the world; and the consequence is that the manufacturing monopoly enjoyed by England for nearly a century is irretrievably broken up.

But the manufacturing monopoly of England is the pivot of the present social system of England. Even while that monopoly lasted, the markets could not keep pace with the increasing productivity of English manufacturers; the decennial crises were the consequence. And new markets are getting scarcer every day, so much so that even the Negroes of the Congo are now to be forced into the civilisation attendant upon Manchester calicos, Staffordshire pottery, and Birmingham hardware. How will it be when Continental, and especially American goods flow in in ever-increasing quantities—when the predominating share, still held by British manufacturers, will become reduced from year to year? Answer, Free Trade, thou universal panacea.

I am not the first to point this out. Already in 1883, at the Southport meeting of the British Association, Mr. Inglis Palgrave, the President of the Economic section, stated plainly that "the days of great trade profits in England were over, and there was a pause in the progress of several great branches of industrial labour. The country might almost be said to be entering the non-progressive state."

But what is to be the consequence? Capitalist production cannot stop. It must go on increasing and expanding, or it must die. Even a Report of the Fifty-Third Meeting of the British Association for the Advancement of Science; held at Southport in September 1883, now the mere reduction of England's lion's share in the supply of the world's markets means stagnation, distress, excess of capital here, excess of unemployed work-people there. What will it be when the increase of yearly production is brought to a complete stop?

Here is the vulnerable place, the heel of Achilles, for capitalistic production. Its very basis is the necessity of constant expansion, and this constant expansion now becomes impossible. It ends in a deadlock. Every year England is brought nearer face to face with the question: either the country must go to pieces, or capitalist production must. Which is it to be?

And the working-class? If even under the unparalleled commercial and industrial expansion, from 1848 to 1868, they have had to undergo such misery; if even then the great bulk of them experienced at best but a temporary improvement of their condition, while only a small, privileged, "protected" minority was permanently benefited, what will it be when this dazzling period is brought finally

The truth is this: during the period of England's industrial monopoly the English working-class have, to a certain extent, shared in the benefits of the monopoly. These benefits were very unequally parcelled out amongst them; the privileged minority pocketed most, but even the great mass had, at least, a temporary share now and then. And that is the reason why, since the dying-out of Owenism, there has been no Socialism in England.

to a close; when the present dreary stagnation shall not only become intensified, but this, its intensified condition, shall become the permanent and normal state of English trade?

The truth is this: during the period of England's industrial monopoly the English working-class have, to a certain extent, shared in the benefits of the monopoly. These benefits were very unequally parcelled out amongst them; the privileged minority pocketed most, but even the great mass had, at least, a temporary share now and then. And that is the reason why, since the dying-out of Owenism, there has been no Socialism in England. With the breakdown of that monopoly, the English working-class will lose that privileged position; it will find itself generally—the privileged and leading minority not excepted—on a level with its fellow-workers abroad. And that is the reason why there will be Socialism again in England.

MEOB pp. 24–31

> **With the breakdown of that monopoly, the English working-class will lose that privileged position; it will find itself generally—the privileged and leading minority not excepted—on a level with its fellow-workers abroad. And that is the reason why there will be Socialism again in England.**

Letter from Engels to Bebel

London, October 28th, 1885.

The chronic depression in all the decisive branches of industry also still continues unbroken here, in France and in America. Especially in iron and cotton. It is an unheard-of situation, though entirely the inevitable result of the capitalist system: such colossal over-production that it cannot even bring things to a crisis! The over-production of disposable capital seeking investment is so great that the rate of discount here actually fluctuates between 1 and 1½ per cent per annum, and for money invested in short-term credits, which can be paid off or called in any day (money on call) one can hardly get ½ per cent per annum. But by choosing to invest his money in this way rather than in new industrial undertakings the money capitalist is admitting how rotten the whole business looks to him. And this fear of new investments and old-time speculation, which already manifested itself in the crisis of 1867, is the main reason why things are not brought to an acute crisis. But it will have to come in the end all the same, and then it will make an end of the old trade unions here, let us hope. These unions have nonchalantly retained the craft character which stuck to them from the first and which is becoming more unbearable every day. No doubt you suppose that the engineers, joiners, bricklayers, etc., will admit any worker into their trade without more ado? Not at all. Whoever wants admission must first have been attached as an apprentice for a period of years (usually seven) to some worker belonging to the union. This was intended to keep the number of workers limited, but had no point at all except that it brought in money to the apprentice's master, for which he actually did nothing in return. This was tolerable up to 1848. But since then the colossal growth of industry has produced a class of workers of whom there are as many or more as there are "skilled" workers in the trade unions and whose performance is as good as that of the "skilled" workers or better, but who can never become members. These people have been virtually brought up on the craft rules of the trade unions. But do you suppose the unions ever dreamt of doing away with this silly bunk? Not in the least. I cannot recall having read of a single proposal of the kind at a Trade Union Congress. The fools want to reform society to suit themselves but not to reform themselves to suit the development of society. They cling to their traditional superstition, which does them nothing but harm, instead of getting quit of the rubbish and thus doubling their numbers and their power and really becoming again what at present they daily become less—associations of all the workers in a trade against the capitalists. This I think will explain many things to you in the behaviour of these privileged workers.

MESC p. 386

Letter from Engels to Sorge

London, December 7th, 1889.

Here one can see that it is by no means easy to drill ideas into a big nation in a doctrinaire and dogmatic way, even if one has the best of theories, developed out of its own conditions of life, and even if the tutors are relatively better than those of the SLP.* The movement has now got going at last and I believe for good. But it is not directly socialist, and those Englishmen who have understood our theory best remain outside it: Hyndman because he is an incurable intriguer and jealous, too; Bax because he is a bookworm. Formally the movement is at the moment a Trade-Union movement, but totally different from that of the old Trade Unions, the skilled labourers, the aristocracy of labour.

The people are throwing themselves into the job in quite a different spirit, are leading far huger masses into the fight, are shaking society much more deeply, are putting forward much more far-reaching demands: eight-hour day, general federation of all organisations, complete solidarity. Thanks to Tussy, the Gas Workers' and General Labourers' Union has formed women's branches for the first time. Moreover, the people themselves regard their immediate demands as only provisional, although they do not know as yet what final aim they are working for. But this dim idea is strongly enough rooted to make them choose only avowed Socialists as their leaders. Like everyone else they will have to learn by their own experiences and the consequences of their own mistakes. But as, unlike the old Trade Unions, they greet every suggestion of

---

* *Socialist Labour Party, USA.*

an identity of interests between capital and labour with scorn and ridicule this will not take very long …

The most repulsive thing here is the bourgeois "respectability" bred into the bones of the workers. The social division of society into innumerable gradations, each recognised without question, each with its own pride but also its inborn respect for its "betters" and "superiors," is so old and firmly established that the bourgeois still find it pretty easy to get their bait accepted. I am not at all sure, for instance, that John Burns is not secretly prouder of his popularity with Cardinal Manning, the Lord Mayor and the bourgeoisie in general than of his popularity with his own class. And Champion an ex-Lieutenant—intrigued years ago with bourgeois, and especially with conservative, elements, preached Socialism at the parsons' Church Congress, etc. Even Tom Mann, whom I regard as the finest of them, is fond of mentioning that he will be lunching with the Lord Mayor. If one compares this with the French, one can see what a revolution is good for, after all.

MESC p. 407
MEOB p. 567

Letter from Engels to Sorge

London, April 19th, 1890.

In a country with such an old political and labour movement there is always a tremendous heap of traditionally inherited rubbish which has to be got rid of by degrees. There are the prejudices of the skilled Unions—Engineers, Bricklayers, Carpenters and Joiners, Type Compositors, etc.—which have all to be broken down; the petty jealousies of the particular trades, which become intensified in the hands and heads of the leaders to the point of direct hostility and underhand struggle; there are the mutually conflicting ambitions and intrigues of the leaders: one wants to get into Parliament and so does somebody else, a third wants to get into the County Council or on the School Board, a fourth wants to organise a general central body

In short, anyone who looks only at the surface would say it was all confusion and personal quarrels. But under the surface the movement is going on, is embracing ever wider sections and mostly just among the hitherto stagnant lowest strata.

comprising all workers, a fifth to start a paper, a sixth a club, etc., etc. In short, there is friction galore. And among them is the Socialist League, which looks down on everything that is not directly revolutionary (which means here in England as in your country: all who do not limit themselves to making phrases and otherwise doing nothing), and the Federation, which still behaves as if all except themselves were asses and bunglers, although it is precisely owing to the new impetus lent to the movement that they have succeeded in getting some following again. In short, anyone who looks only at the surface would say it was all confusion and personal quarrels. But under the surface the movement is going on, is embracing ever wider sections and mostly just among the hitherto stagnant lowest strata. The day is no longer far off when this mass will suddenly find itself, when it will dawn upon it that it itself is this colossal mass in motion, and when that day comes short work will be made of all the rascality and wrangling.

MESC p. 411
MEOB p. 570

Letter from Engels to Kautsky

Ryde, September 4th, 1892.

If you had been here during the last elections you would talk differently about the Fabians.* In our tactics one thing is thoroughly established for all modern countries and times: to bring the workers to the point of forming their own party, independent and opposed to all bourgeois parties. During the last elections the English workers, for the first time and perhaps still only instinctively, pressed by the course of events, took a decided step in this direction; and this step has been surprisingly successful and has contributed more to the development of the minds of the workers than any other event of the last twenty years. And what did the Fabians do, not just this or that Fabian but the society as a whole? It preached and practised: affiliation of the workers to the Liberals, and what was to be expected happened: the Liberals assigned them four seats that it was impossible to win and the Fabian candidates conspicuously failed. The paradoxical belletrist Shaw—very talented and witty as a belletrist but absolutely useless as an economist and politician, although honest and not a careerist—wrote to Bebel that if they did not follow this policy of forcing their candidates on the Liberals they would reap nothing but defeat and disgrace (as if defeat were not often more honourable than victory) and now they have pursued their policy and have reaped both.

That is the crux of the whole matter. At a time when the workers for the first time come out independently the Fabian Society

---

* *The Fabian Society was formed in 1884. In 1900 the society joined the Labour Party.*

advises them to remain the tail of the Liberals. ...

You see something unfinished in the Fabian Society. On the contrary, this crowd is only too finished: a clique of bourgeois "Socialists" of diverse calibres, from careerists to sentimental Socialists and philanthropists, united only by their fear of the threatening rule of the workers and doing all in their power to spike this danger by making their own leadership secure, the leadership exercised by the "eddicated." If afterwards they admit a few workers into their central board in order that they may play there the role of the worker Albert of 1848, the role of a constantly outvoted minority, this should not deceive anyone.

The means employed by the Fabian Society are just the same as those of the corrupt parliamentary politicians: money, intrigues, careerism. That is, English careerism, according to which it is self-understood that every political party (only among the workers it is supposed to be different!) pays its agents in some way or other or rewards them with posts. These people are immersed up to their necks in the intrigues of the Liberal Party, hold Liberal Party jobs, as for instance Sidney Webb, who in general is a genuine British politician. These gentry do everything that the workers have to be warned against.

MESC p. 446
MEOB p. 575

Letter from Engels to Sorge

London, January 18th, 1893.

This Socialism of [the Fabians] is then represented as an extreme but inevitable consequence of bourgeois Liberalism; hence their tactics of not resolutely fighting the Liberals as adversaries but of pushing them on towards Socialist conclusions and therefore of intriguing with them, of permeating Liberalism with Socialism, of not putting up Socialist candidates against the Liberals but of fastening them on to the Liberals ...

The Fabians are a gang of careerists here in London who have understanding enough to realise the inevitability of the social revolution, but who could not possibly entrust this gigantic task to the raw proletariat alone and are therefore kind enough to put themselves at the head. Fear of the revolution is their fundamental principle. They are the "eddicated" par excellence. Their Socialism is municipal Socialism; not the nation but the municipality is to become the owner of the means of production, at any rate for the time being. This Socialism of theirs is then represented as an extreme but inevitable consequence of bourgeois Liberalism; hence their tactics of not resolutely fighting the Liberals as adversaries but of pushing them on towards Socialist conclusions and therefore of intriguing with them, of permeating Liberalism with Socialism, of not putting up Socialist candidates against the Liberals but of fastening them on to the Liberals, of forcing them upon them, or deceiving them into taking them. That in the course of this process they either are lied to and deceived themselves or else belie Socialism, they do not of course realise.

With great industry they have produced amid all sorts of rubbish some good propagandist writings as well, in fact the best of the kind which the English have produced. But as soon as they come to their specific tactics of hushing up the class struggle it all turns putrid. Hence too their fanatical hatred of Marx and all of us—because of the class struggle.

MESC p. 453
MEOB p. 578

Letter from Engels to Plekhanov

London, May 21st, 1894.

One is indeed driven to despair by these English workers with their sense of imaginary national superiority, with their essentially bourgeois ideas and viewpoints, with their "practical" narrow-mindedness, with the parliamentary corruption which has seriously infected the leaders. But things are moving none the less. The only thing is that the "practical" English will be the last to arrive, but when they do arrive their contribution will weigh quite heavy in the scale.

MEOB p. 583

> One is indeed driven to despair by these English workers with their sense of imaginary national superiority, with their essentially bourgeois ideas and viewpoints, with their "practical" narrow-mindedness, with the parliamentary corruption which has seriously infected the leaders.

ALSO AVAILABLE FROM KERSPLEBEDEB

Turning Money into Rebellion: The Unlikely Story of Denmark's Revolutionary Bank Robbers

ed. Gabriel Kuhn • 9781604863161

224 pages • $20.00

One of the most captivating chapters from the European anti-imperialist milieu of the 1970s and '80s; the Blekingegade Group had emerged from a communist organization whose analysis of the metropolitan labor aristocracy led them to develop an illegal Third Worldist practice, sending millions of dollars acquired in spectacular heists to Third World liberation movements.

The book includes historical documents, illustrations, and an exclusive interview with Torkil Lauesen and Jan Weimann, two of the group's longest-standing members. It is a compelling tale of turning radical theory into action and concerns analysis and strategy as much as morality and political practice. Perhaps most importantly, it revolves around the cardinal question of revolutionary politics: What to do, and how to do it?

KERSPLEBEDEB, CP 63560, CCCP VAN HORNE, MONTREAL, QUEBEC, CANADA H3W 3H8

ALSO AVAILABLE FROM KERSPLEBEDEB

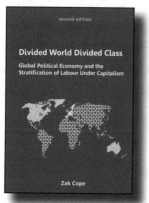

Divided World Divided Class: Global Political Economy and the Stratification of Labour Under Capitalism SECOND EDITION

Zak Cope • 978189494-6681
460 pages • $24.95

Charting the history of the "labour aristocracy" in the capitalist world system, from its roots in colonialism to its birth and eventual maturation into a full-fledged middle class in the age of imperialism. Demonstrating not only how redistribution of income derived from super-exploitation has allowed for the amelioration of class conflict in the wealthy capitalist countries, but also that the exorbitant "super-wage" paid to workers there has meant the disappearance of a domestic vehicle for socialism, an exploited working class. Rather, in its place is a deeply conservative metropolitan workforce committed to maintaining, and even extending, its privileged position through imperialism.

KERSPLEBEDEB, CP 63560, CCCP VAN HORNE, MONTREAL, QUEBEC, CANADA H3W 3H8

ALSO AVAILABLE FROM KERSPLEBEDEB

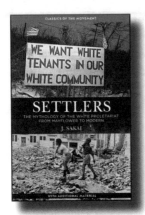

Settlers: The Mythology of the White Proletariat from Mayflower to Modern

J. Sakai • 978162963-0373
456 pages • $20.00

The United States is a country built on the theft of Indigenous lands and Afrikan labor, on the robbery of the northern third of Mexico, the colonization of Puerto Rico, and the expropriation of the Asian working class, with each of these crimes being accompanied by violence. In fact, America's white citizenry have never supported themselves but have always resorted to exploitation and theft, culminating in acts of genocide to maintain their culture and way of life. This movement classic lays it all out, taking us through this painful but important history.

This new edition includes "Cash & Genocide: The True Story of Japanese-American Reparations" and an interview with author J. Sakai by Ernesto Aguilar.

KERSPLEBEDEB, CP 63560, CCCP VAN HORNE, MONTREAL, QUEBEC, CANADA H3W 3H8

ALSO AVAILABLE FROM KERSPLEBEDEB

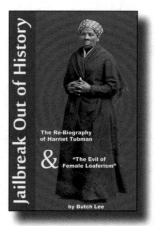

Jailbreak Out of History: the Re-Biography of Harriet Tubman & "The Evil of Female Loaferism" SECOND EDITION

Butch Lee • 9781894946704
169 pages • $14.95

The anticolonial struggles waged by New Afrikan women were central to the unfolding of 19th century amerika, both during and "after" slavery. "The Re-Biography of Harriet Tubman" recounts the life and politics of Harriet Tubman, who waged and eventually lead the war against the capitalist slave system. "The Evil of Female Loaferism" details New Afrikan women's attempts immediately after the Civil War to withdraw from and evade capitalist colonialism, an unofficial but massive labor strike which threw the capitalists North and South into a panic. The ruling class response consisted of the "Black Codes," Jim Crow, re-enslavement through prison labor, mass violence, and ... the establishment of a neo-colonial Black patriarchy, whose task was to make New Afrikan women subordinate to New Afrikan men just as New Afrika was supposed to be subordinate to white amerika.

KERSPLEBEDEB, CP 63560, CCCP VAN HORNE, MONTREAL, QUEBEC, CANADA H3W 3H8

KERSPLEBEDEB

Since 1998 Kersplebedeb has been an important source of radical literature and agit prop materials.

The project has a non-exclusive focus on anti-patriarchal and anti-imperialist politics, framed within an anticapitalist perspective. A special priority is given to writings regarding armed struggle in the metropole and the continuing struggles of political prisoners and prisoners of war.

Kersplebedeb can be contacted at:

> Kersplebedeb
> CP 63560, CCCP Van Horne
> Montreal, Quebec
> Canada H3W 3H8
>
> email: info@kersplebedeb.com
> web: www.kersplebedeb.com
> www.leftwingbooks.net

Kersplebedeb